Better
TOGETHER
HELPING COUPLES CREATE GREAT MARRIAGES

Design by: Jessica Amsberry

ISBN 9781635820744

FIRST EDITION

THIS BOOK WILL HELP YOU SELECT THE READINGS AND PRAYERS FOR YOUR CEREMONY.

To make your selections and share them with your priest or deacon, you may fill out the forms included in this book or visit the link below to complete the forms and have them sent electronically.

DynamicCatholic.com/CeremonyForm

HOW TO USE THIS RESOURCE

What a special day you are about to celebrate!

Choosing the prayers and readings for your wedding day is a great opportunity to build a ceremony that uniquely shares your dreams for your marriage. This resource will guide you through the process of shaping your wedding ceremony in conjunction with your priest or deacon. Most of all, you have many options for the readings and prayers to incorporate into your wedding ceremony. This booklet will provide those options and help you choose the ones that work best for you.

The Church offers three types of wedding ceremonies (called "the Rite of Marriage").

Before choosing your readings and prayers, you will need to decide which form of the Rite of Marriage best fits your needs. Your priest or deacon can help you determine which one to select.

Rite 1: **THE ORDER OF CELEBRATING MATRIMONY WITHIN MASS:** Also called a Nuptial Mass, this form can be used when two baptized Catholics are getting married. This Rite of Marriage enables you couple to share the gift of the Eucharist together. See **page 1** for the prayer options for this Rite of Marriage.

Rite 2: **THE ORDER OF CELEBRATING MATRIMONY WITHOUT MASS:** This form is used if one of you is a baptized non-Catholic Christian. It is also used if a priest is not available to celebrate the Mass and a deacon officiates instead. Some couples will elect to use this form if their families or a large number of guests are not Catholic. See **page 31** for the prayer options.

Rite 3: **THE ORDER OF CELEBRATING MATRIMONY BETWEEN A CATHOLIC AND A CATECHUMEN OR A NON-CHRISTIAN:** This form is used when a Catholic marries an unbaptized person or catechumen preparing for baptism. The couple must receive permission from the local bishop. See **page 57** for the prayer options for this Rite of Marriage.

Once you know which Rite of Marriage you are using, turn to the pages listed above to see your options for the various prayers. The same Bible readings are used regardless of which Rite of Marriage you select, and can be found on page 73.

Spend time with your spouse-to-be reading through these options. Once you have made your selections, add them to the Selection Form that corresponds to the Rite of Marriage you are using. You can find the Selection Forms in the back of this book in the Appendix. After completing the form, tear it out and give it to your priest or deacon.

If you would rather share your selections via email, visit **DynamicCatholic.com/CeremonyForm** to send an electronic version of the Selection Form to your priest or deacon.

As the options for prayers may vary by parish, be sure to connect with your parish before making your selections. Keep in mind that if your wedding falls on a Sunday, within Lent, or on certain solemnities and feast days, your options for the readings and prayers may vary. Your priest or deacon will help you determine if there are any limitations or special circumstances.

At the end of this resource, you will find Frequently Asked Questions and featured articles from various resources to nourish you as you begin this lifelong journey together.

INTRODUCTION

The most beautiful part of your wedding day is the ceremony itself. After all, it is the time you officially become husband and wife! Therefore, selecting the readings and prayers for the ceremony is an important decision you will make when planning your big day.

Just as it is fun to choose the decorations, the venues, and the band, you can have fun crafting the ceremony by choosing readings and prayers that speak to you and serve as an expression of the hopes and dreams you have for your marriage. Choose the readings that describe your relationship with each other, your relationship with God, and how you want your marriage to look. You can then share this vision with your loved ones in a deeply personal way.

God wants to be with you in every moment of your marriage.

He wants to bless your marriage and accompany you and your spouse through the journey you are beginning together. As you build your wedding ceremony by intentionally selecting the readings, prayers, music, celebrants, etc., invite God to guide you through the process.

TABLE OF CONTENTS

God wants to be with you in every moment of your marriage.

The Order of Celebrating Matrimony **Within Mass**

RITE 1

○ *Indicates a step in your planning process.*

THE INTRODUCTORY RITE

The Introductory Rite begins the wedding. The priest or deacon, groom, parents, bridal party, and bride enter the church. The priest or deacon welcomes them either before they enter the church or after everyone has reached their seats and the bride and groom are standing at the altar. He then greets the congregation and begins the ceremony.

THE COLLECT

The Collect is prayed after the procession and greeting. It brings everyone together in prayer and prepares them for the liturgy.

OPTION 1

Be attentive to our prayers, O Lord,
and in your kindness
pour out your grace on these your servants N. and N.,
that, coming together before your altar,
they may be confirmed in love for one another.
Through our Lord Jesus Christ, your Son,
who lives and reigns with you in the unity of the Holy Spirit,
one God, for ever and ever.

OPTION 2

Please note: *This option may not be used if Option 1 of the Nuptial Blessing on page 23 is selected.*

O God, who consecrated the bond of Marriage
by so great a mystery
that in the wedding covenant you foreshadow
the Sacrament of Christ and his Church,

grant, we pray, to these your servants,
that what they receive in faith
they may live out in deeds.
Through our Lord Jesus Christ, your Son,
who lives and reigns with you in the unity of the Holy Spirit,
one God, for ever and ever.

OPTION 3

O God, who in creating the human race
willed that man and wife should be one,
join, we pray, in a bond of inseparable love
these your servants who are to be united in the covenant of Marriage,
so that, as you make their love fruitful,
they may become, by your grace, witnesses to charity itself.
Through our Lord Jesus Christ, your Son,
Who lives and reigns with you in the unity of the Holy Spirit,
One God, for ever and ever.

OPTION 4

Grant, we pray, almighty God,
that these your servants,
now to be joined by the Sacrament of Matrimony,
may grow in the faith they profess
and enrich your Church with faithful offspring.
Through our Lord Jesus Christ, your Son,
who lives and reigns with you in the unity of the Holy Spirit,
one God, for ever and ever.

OPTION 5

Be attentive to our prayers, O Lord,
And in your kindness uphold
what you have established for the increase of the human race,

so that the union you have created
may be kept safe by your assistance.
Through our Lord Jesus Christ, your Son,
Who lives and reigns with you in the unity of the Holy Spirit,
One God, for ever and ever.

OPTION 6

O God, who since the beginning of the world
have blessed the increase of offspring,
show favor to our supplications
and pour forth the help of your blessing
on these your servants N. and N.,
so that in the union of Marriage
they may be bound together
in mutual affection,
in likeness of mind,
and in shared holiness.
Through our Lord Jesus Christ, your Son,
who lives and reigns with you in the unity of the Holy Spirit,
one God, for ever and ever.

THE LITURGY OF THE WORD

As a couple, you will choose two or three readings, plus a Responsorial
Psalm, to incorporate in your ceremony. After the readings, the priest
or deacon will deliver a homily that draws from these readings in the
context of the celebration of matrimony.

_____

Below are summaries of the readings. At least one reading must explicitly reference marriage. These are marked with a *. For the full readings, see page 73.

FIRST READING

*OPTION 1 – Genesis 1:26–28, 31a: Man and woman were created for one another. This story of the creation shows the beauty and complementarity of the relationship between man and woman.

*OPTION 2 – Genesis 2:18–24: This reading celebrates the special bond between a man and woman. It is a beautiful moment when Adam sees Eve for the first time, exclaiming, "This one, at last, is bone of my bones and flesh of my flesh."

*OPTION 3 – Genesis 24: 48–51, 58–67: The story of Rebekah and Isaac's marriage celebrates marriage as a gift from God. Rebekah gives her consent and follows the will of God in marrying Isaac. This passage includes a blessing for the bride.

*OPTION 4 – Tobit 7:6–14: Sarah and Tobiah seek peace and prosperity on their marriage. After facing several obstacles, they are united as husband and wife. In times of suffering, they find joy in following God's plan.

OPTION 5 – Tobit 8:4b–8: This reading captures a very special and intimate moment. Tobiah and Sarah begin their wedding night together in prayer. They place God at the center of their marriage and ask him to bless their life together.

*OPTION 6 – Proverbs 31:10–13, 19–20, 30–31: Finding the woman you want to spend the rest of your life with is a beautiful thing. Someone who will challenge you, serve others, and bring you closer to God.

OPTION 7 – Song of Songs 2:8–10, 14, 16a; 8:6–7a: Song of Songs is a beautiful collection of poems that reflect the intimate words of a lover. This passage voices the desire to be together and the incredible power of love.

*OPTION 8 – Sirach 26:1–4, 13–16: This reading rejoices in the joy a good wife brings to her husband through her thoughtfulness, decency, and virtue.

OPTION 9 – Jeremiah 31:31–32a, 33–34a: This reading shows the love God has for us. God instituted a new covenant in which His love became inscribed in our hearts. Similarly, the covenant of marriage will be a covenant of love between you, your spouse, and God.

Note: *If you are incorporating a First Reading and a Second Reading and your wedding is held during the Easter season, the First Reading should be from the Book of Revelation. Speak with your priest or deacon to make this selection.*

RESPONSORIAL PSALM

OPTION 1 – Psalm 33:12 and 18, 20–21, 22: "The earth is full of the goodness of the Lord."

OPTION 2 – Psalm 34:2–3, 4–5, 6–7, 8–9: "I will bless the Lord at all times." OR "Taste and see the goodness of the Lord."

OPTION 3 – Psalm 103:1–2, 8 and 13, 17–18a: "The Lord is kind and merciful." OR "The Lord's kindness is everlasting to those who fear him."

OPTION 4 – 112:1bc–2, 3–4, 5–7a, 7b–8, 9: "Blessed the man who greatly delights in the Lord's commands." OR "Alleluia."

*OPTION 5 – Psalm 128:1–2, 3, 4–5ac and 6a: "Blessed are those who fear the Lord." OR "See how the Lord blesses those who fear him."

OPTION 6 – Psalm 145:8–9, 10 and 15, 17–18: "How good is the Lord to all."

OPTION 7 – Psalm 148:1–2, 3–4, 9–10, 11–13ab, 13c–14a: "Let all praise the name of the Lord." OR "Alleluia."

SECOND READING

OPTION 1 – Romans 8:31b–35, 37–39: It is only by placing God at the center of everything that we can make sense of life. When we place something or someone else at the center of our lives we set ourselves up for a gnawing dissatisfaction.

OPTION 2 – Romans 12:1–2, 9–18 (long form) OR Romans 12:1–2, 9–13 (short form): The things of this world can distract us in a hundred different ways. But this reading encourages a more radical way of living, with love and God as the center.

OPTION 3 – Romans 15: 1b–3a, 5–7, 13: Love isn't always easy. This reading asks God to help us truly love one another, despite each other's faults.

OPTION 4 – 1 Corinthians 6:13c–15a, 17–20: This reading encourages us to remember that we were made for God, and it is in God that we will flourish.

OPTION 5 – 1 Corinthians 12:31–13:8a: St. Paul's words encourage us to persevere in love. He assures readers that when love is patient, kind, and rejoices with the truth, it endures all things.

OPTION 6 – Ephesians 4:1–6: In this reading, St. Paul encourages us to live the best life that we can, to embrace our own journey, and to bear with one another through love.

*OPTION 7 – Ephesians 5:2a, 21–33 (long form) OR Ephesians 5:2a, 25–32 (short form): Husbands are asked to lay down their entire lives for their wives, and wives are encouraged to show love and respect for their husbands.

OPTION 8 – Philippians 4:4–9: This is an invitation to rejoice, and encouragement to have no anxiety if we put God at the center of our lives. He brings us joy when we focus on whatever is true, honorable, just, pure, lovely, and gracious.

OPTION 9 – Colossians 3:12–17: This reading celebrates a life of character and virtue. It talks about the greatest virtue of love and encourages us to invite Jesus to bring peace and love into our hearts.

OPTION 10 – Hebrews 13:1–4a, 5–6b: Marriage is something worth celebrating and holding in high esteem. Marriage is at its best when both husband and wife seek help in God.

*OPTION 11 – 1 Peter 3:1–9: This reading talks about how true beauty is not found on the outside, but within. It encourages us to exercise compassion and to be a blessing for one another through our conduct.

OPTION 12 – 1 John 3:18–24: Life is full of challenges, but God will always help when we follow his commandment to love one another "in deed and truth."

OPTION 13 – 1 John 4:7–12: This passage encourages us to love one another because God loved us. We receive this gift of love from God and participate in it by loving others.

OPTION 14 – Revelation 19:1, 5–9a: This reading is from the last book of the Bible. It captures John's vision of the wedding feast of the Lamb, of Jesus at the end of time. It is a beautiful way to see how marriage ultimately points us to heaven.

ALLELUIA VERSE

OPTION 1 – 1 John 4:7b: "Everyone who loves is begotten of God and knows God."

OPTION 2 – 1 John 4:8b and 11: "God is love; let us love one another, as God has loved us."

OPTION 3 – 1 John 4:12: "If we love one another, God remains in us and his love is brought to perfection in us."

OPTION 4 – 1 John 4:16: "Whoever remains in love, remains in God and God in him."

OPTION 5 – Psalm 134:3: "May the LORD bless you from Zion, he who made both heaven and earth."

GOSPEL

OPTION 1 – Matthew 5:1–12a: This passage captures Jesus' Sermon on the Mount. He gives a beautiful and powerful vision of a life well lived in the famous Beatitudes.

OPTION 2 – Matthew 5:13–16: Jesus tells his disciples they can have an incredible impact on the world and the people around them if they boldly live out their faith.

OPTION 3 – Matthew 7:21, 24–29 (long form) OR Matthew 7:21, 24–25 (short form): Jesus tells the parable of a man who built his house on rock and a man who built his house on sand. A marriage that puts God at the center is a marriage built on rock.

OPTION 4 – Matthew 19:3–6: Marriage is forever. In this reading, Jesus is questioned about divorce, and he responds saying, "what God has joined together, man must not separate."

OPTION 5 – Matthew 22:35–40: Love is a beautiful thing. And it is our calling. When someone asks Jesus what the greatest commandment is, he replies that the greatest commandment is to love God with all your heart, soul, and mind, and the second is to love your neighbor as yourself.

OPTION 6 – Mark 10:6–9: Jesus celebrates the beauty of the union between man and woman in marriage, and stresses that what God has joined together no one must separate.

OPTION 7 – John 2:1–11: Jesus performs his first miracle at a wedding. His act of turning water into wine symbolizes how God gives in abundance to those who have faith and believe in his goodness.

OPTION 8 – John 15:9–12: As he prepares to leave his disciples and ascend into Heaven, Jesus tells them that the path to complete joy is to love one another as he has loved them. He encourages them (and us) to remain in his love.

OPTION 9 – John 15:12–16: There is no greater love than laying down your life for a friend. Christ laid down his life for us, demonstrating the love of God. Husbands and wives are called to love as Christ loved us by sacrificing for one another and by living selflessly.

OPTION 10 – John 17:20–26 (long form) OR John 17:20–23 (short form): Jesus desires that we will know the love of God the Father and that we will be with him in Heaven. Through your love for one another, you and your spouse will strive to bring each other closer to God and closer to Heaven.

THE CELEBRATION OF MATRIMONY

This is the part of the ceremony where the bride and groom officially become husband and wife. When prompted by the priest or deacon, the bride and groom exchange vows (called "The Exchange of Consent") and pledge their commitment to remain together for the rest of their lives.

THE INTRODUCTION AND QUESTIONS BEFORE CONSENT

After the priest or deacon addresses the couple with the following words, they declare their intentions to marry one another by separately responding to his questions:

Dearly beloved,
you have come together into the house of the Church,
so that in the presence of the Church's minister and the community
your intention to enter into Marriage
may be strengthened by the Lord with a sacred seal.
Christ abundantly blesses the love that binds you.
through a special Sacrament,
he enriches and strengthens
those he has already consecrated by Holy Baptism,
that they may be faithful to each other for ever
and assume all the responsibilities of married life.
And so, in the presence of the Church,
I ask you to state your intentions.
N. and N., have you come here to enter into Marriage
without coercion,
freely and wholeheartedly?

The bride and groom each respond: I have.

Are you prepared, as you follow the path of Marriage,
to love and honor each other
for as long as you both shall live?

The bride and groom each respond: I am.

Are you prepared to accept children lovingly from God
and to bring them up
according to the law of Christ and his Church?

The bride and groom each respond: I am.

THE CONSENT

You and your fiancé will exchange marriage vows, either with full recitation
or by simply saying "I do" after the priest or deacon says the following:

Since it is your intention to enter the covenant of Holy Matrimony, join your
right hands and declare your consent before God and his Church.

OPTION 1

The groom says:
I, N., take you, N., to be my wife.
I promise to be faithful to you,
in good times and in bad,
in sickness and in health,
to love you and to honor you
all the days of my life.

The bride says:
I, N., take you, N., to be my husband.
I promise to be faithful to you,

in good times and in bad,
in sickness and in health,
to love you and to honor you
all the days of my life.

The groom says:
I, N., take you, N., for my lawful wife,
to have and to hold, from this day forward,
for better, for worse,
for richer, for poorer,
in sickness and in health,
to love and to cherish
until death do us part.

The bride says:
I, N., take you, N., for my lawful husband,
to have and to hold, from this day forward,
for better, for worse,
for richer, for poorer,
in sickness and in health,
to love and to cherish
until death do us part.

N., do you take N., to be your wife?
Do you promise to be faithful to her
in good times and in bad,
in sickness and in health,
to love her and to honor her
all the days of your life?

The groom responds: I do.

N., do you take N., to be your husband?
Do you promise to be faithful to him
in good times and in bad,
in sickness and in health,
to love him and to honor him
all the days of your life?

The bride responds: I do.

OPTION 4

N., do you take N. for your lawful wife,
to have and to hold, from this day forward,
for better, for worse,
for richer, for poorer,
in sickness and in health,
to love and to cherish
until death do you part?

The groom responds: I do.

N., do you take N. for your lawful husband,
to have and to hold, from this day forward,
for better, for worse,
for richer, for poorer,
in sickness and in health,
to love and to cherish
until death do you part?

The bride responds: I do.

THE RECEPTION OF CONSENT

The priest or deacon serves as the Church's witness of your marriage. In this prayer, the priest or deacon acknowledges the consent of the bride and groom.

OPTION 1

May the Lord in his kindness strengthen the consent
you have declared before the Church,
and graciously bring to fulfillment his blessing within you.
What God joins together, let no one put asunder.

OPTION 2

May the God of Abraham, the God of Isaac, the God of Jacob,
the God who joined together our first parents in paradise,
strengthen and bless in Christ
the consent you have declared before the Church,
so that what God joins together, no one may put asunder.

THE BLESSING AND GIVING OF RINGS

The priest or deacon says a blessing over your rings before you place them on each other's ring finger as a symbol of your marriage vows.

OPTION 1

May the Lord bless these rings,
which you will give to each other
as a sign of love and fidelity.

Bless, O Lord, these rings,
which we bless in your name,
so that those who wear them
may remain entirely faithful to each other,
abide in peace and in your will,
and live always in mutual charity.
Through Christ our Lord.

Bless and sanctify your servants
in their love, O Lord,
and let these rings, a sign of their faithfulness,
remind them of their love for one another.
Through Christ our Lord.

THE BLESSING AND GIVING OF THE *ARRAS*

If the occasion suggests, the rite of blessing and giving of the *arras* (coins) may take place after the blessing and giving of rings. Speak with your priest or deacon if you are interested in integrating this into your ceremony.

THE UNIVERSAL PRAYER

Also known as the Prayer of the Faithful, this is a collection of intercessory prayers. Your priest or deacon will have several options available for you to choose from. It may also be possible for you to craft your own Universal Prayer with the assistance of your priest or deacon.

THE LITURGY OF THE EUCHARIST

If you are using The Order of Celebrating Matrimony Within Mass, the priest will prepare the altar and the offerings of bread and wine, which will soon become the Body and Blood of Jesus. Receiving Holy Communion with your beloved (now your spouse) is a wonderful way to celebrate the union you have just entered into with one another.

_____

THE PRAYER OVER THE GIFTS

The priest says a prayer over the bread and wine, asking God to guide you in your marriage.

OPTION 1

Receive, we pray, O Lord,
the offering made on the occasion
of this sealing of the sacred bond of Marriage,
and, just as your goodness is its origin,
may your providence guide its course.
Through Christ our Lord.

OPTION 2

Receive in your kindness, Lord,
the offerings we bring in gladness before you,
and in your fatherly love
watch over those you have joined in a sacramental covenant.
Through Christ our Lord.

Show favor to our supplications, O Lord,
and receive with a kindly countenance
the oblations we offer for these your servants,
joined now in a holy covenant,
that through these mysteries
they may be strengthened
in love for one another and for you.
Through Christ our Lord.

THE PREFACE

The Preface proclaims God's goodness. The priest leads all present in
offering their praises to God. After the Preface and the Sanctus (Holy,
Holy, Holy), the priest consecrates the bread and wine, during which they
become the Body and Blood of Jesus.

OPTION 1

It is truly right and just, our duty and our salvation,
always and everywhere to give you thanks,
Lord, holy Father, almighty and eternal God.
For you have forged the covenant of Marriage
as a sweet yoke of harmony
and an unbreakable bond of peace,
so that the chaste and fruitful love of holy Matrimony
may serve to increase the children you adopt as your own.

By your providence and grace, O Lord,
you accomplish the wonder of this twofold design:
that, while the birth of children brings beauty to the world,
their rebirth in Baptism gives increase to the Church,
through Christ our Lord.

Through him, with the Angels and all the Saints,
we sing the hymn of your praise,
as without end we acclaim:

It is truly right and just, our duty and our salvation,
always and everywhere to give you thanks,
Lord, holy Father, almighty and eternal God.

For in him you have made a new covenant with your people,
so that, as you have redeemed man and woman
by the mystery of Christ's Death and Resurrection,
so in Christ you might make them partakers of divine nature
and joint heirs with him of heavenly glory.

In the union of husband and wife
you give a sign of Christ's loving gift of grace,
so that the Sacrament we celebrate
might draw us back more deeply
into the wondrous design of your love.

And so, with the Angels and all the Saints,
we praise you, and without end we acclaim:

It is truly right and just, our duty and our salvation,
always and everywhere to give you thanks,
Lord, holy Father, almighty and eternal God.

For you willed that the human race,
created by the gift of your goodness,
should be raised to such high dignity

that in the union of husband and wife
you might bestow a true image of your love.

For those you created out of charity
you call to the law of charity without ceasing
and grant them a share in your eternal charity.
And so, the Sacrament of holy Matrimony,
as the abiding sign of your own love,
consecrates the love of man and woman,
through Christ our Lord.

Through him, with the Angels and all the Saints,
we sing the hymn of your praise,
as without end we acclaim:

THE BLESSING AND PLACING OF THE *LAZO* OR VEIL

According to local customs, the rite of blessing and placing of the *lazo*
(wedding garland) or of the veil may take place before the Nuptial Blessing.
You and your spouse remain kneeling. If the *lazo* has not been placed earlier,
it may be placed at this time. Alternatively, a veil is placed over the head
of the wife and the shoulders of the husband. This symbolizes the bond
that unites them. Speak with your priest or deacon if you are interested in
integrating this into your ceremony.

THE NUPTIAL BLESSING

The Nuptial Blessing, split into two parts with a moment of silence in
between, is prayed aloud by the priest after the Lord's Prayer (the Our
Father). It is a beautiful moment after the couple has exchanged vows to
ask God to bless them and their marriage.

Part I of The Nuptial Blessing

Words appearing in parenthesis are omitted if the bride and/or groom will not be receiving Communion.

OPTION 1

Dear brothers and sisters,
let us humbly pray to the Lord
that on these his servants, now married in Christ,
he may mercifully pour out
the blessing of his grace
and make of one heart in love
(by the Sacrament of Christ's Body and Blood)
those he has joined by a holy covenant.

OPTION 2

Now let us humbly invoke God's blessing
upon this bride and groom,
that in his kindness he may favor with his help
those on whom he has bestowed the Sacrament of Matrimony.

OPTION 3

Let us pray to the Lord for this bride and groom,
who come to the altar as they begin their married life,
that (partaking of the Body and Blood of Christ)
they may always be bound together by love for one another.

OPTION 4

Let us humbly invoke by our prayers, dear brothers and sisters,
God's blessing upon this bride and groom,
that in his kindness he may favor with his help
those on whom he has bestowed the
Sacrament of Matrimony.

Part II of The Nuptial Blessing

Words appearing in parenthesis may be omitted if the bride and groom are beyond childbearing years, or if other circumstances suggest their omission.

OPTION 1

Please note: *This option may not be used if Option 2 of the Collect on page 3 is selected.*

O God, who by your mighty power
created all things out of nothing,
and, when you had set in place
the beginnings of the universe,
formed man and woman in your own image,
making the woman an inseparable helpmate to the man,
that they might no longer be two, but one flesh,
and taught that what you were pleased to make one
must never be divided;

O God, who consecrated the bond of Marriage
by so great a mystery
that in the wedding covenant you foreshadowed
the Sacrament of Christ and his Church;
O God, by whom woman is joined to man
and the companionship they had in the beginning
is endowed with the one blessing
not forfeited by original sin
nor washed away by the flood.
Look now with favor on these your servants,
joined together in Marriage,
who ask to be strengthened by your blessing.
Send down on them the grace of the Holy Spirit
and pour your love into their hearts,
that they may remain faithful in the Marriage covenant.
May the grace of love and peace

abide in your daughter N.,
and let her always follow the example of those holy women
whose praises are sung in the Scriptures.
May her husband entrust his heart to her,
so that, acknowledging her as his equal
and his joint heir to the life of grace,
he may show her due honor
and cherish her always
with the love that Christ has for his Church.

And now, Lord, we implore you:
may these your servants
hold fast to the faith and keep your commandments;
made one in the flesh,
may they be blameless in all they do;
and with the strength that comes from the Gospel,
may they bear true witness to Christ before all;
(may they be blessed with children,
and prove themselves virtuous parents,
who live to see their children's children).
And grant that,
reaching at last together the fullness of years
for which they hope,
they may come to the life of the blessed
in the Kingdom of Heaven.
Through Christ our Lord.

OPTION 2

Holy Father,
who formed man in your own image,
male and female you created them,

so that as husband and wife, united in body and heart,
they might fulfill their calling in the world;

O God, who, to reveal the great design you formed in your love,
willed that the love of spouses for each other
should foreshadow the covenant you graciously made with your people,
so that, by fulfillment of the sacramental sign,
the mystical marriage of Christ with his Church
might become manifest
in the union of husband and wife among your faithful;

Graciously stretch out your right hand
over these your servants (N. and N.), we pray,
and pour into their hearts the power of the Holy Spirit.

Grant, O Lord,
that, as they enter upon this sacramental union,
they may share with one another the gifts of your love
and, by being for each other a sign of your presence,
become one heart and one mind.

May they also sustain, O Lord, by their deeds
the home they are forming
(and prepare their children
to become members of your heavenly household
by raising them in the way of the Gospel).

Graciously crown with your blessings your daughter N.,
so that, by being a good wife (and mother),
she may bring warmth to her home with a love that is pure
and adorn it with welcoming graciousness.

Bestow a heavenly blessing also, O Lord,
on N., your servant,
that he may be a worthy, good and
faithful husband (and a provident father).

Grant, holy Father,
that, desiring to approach your table
as a couple joined in Marriage in your presence,
they may one day have the joy
of taking part in your great banquet in heaven.
Through Christ our Lord.

OPTION 3

Holy Father, maker of the whole world,
who created man and woman in your own image
and willed that their union be crowned with your blessing,
we humbly beseech you for these your servants,
who are joined today in the Sacrament of Matrimony.

May your abundant blessing, Lord,
come down upon this bride, N.,
and upon N., her companion for life,
and may the power of your Holy Spirit
set their hearts aflame from on high,
so that, living out together the gift of Matrimony,
they may (adorn their family with children
and) enrich the Church.

In happiness may they praise you, O Lord,
in sorrow may they seek you out;
may they have the joy of your presence
to assist them in their toil,
and know that you are near

to comfort them in their need;
let them pray to you in the holy assembly
and bear witness to you in the world,
and after a happy old age,
together with the circle of friends that surrounds them,
may they come to the Kingdom of Heaven.
Through Christ our Lord.

THE PRAYER AFTER COMMUNION

The priest says a prayer of thanksgiving after everyone receives Communion.
Words appearing in parenthesis are omitted if the bride and/or groom will
not be receiving Communion.

OPTION 1

By the power of this sacrifice, O Lord,
accompany with your loving favor
what in your providence you have instituted,
so as to make of one heart in love
those you have already joined in this holy union
(and replenished with the one Bread and the one Chalice).
Through Christ our Lord.

OPTION 2

Having been made partakers at your table,
we pray, O Lord,
that those who are united by the Sacrament of Marriage
may always hold fast to you
and proclaim your name to the world.
Through Christ our Lord.

Grant, we pray, almighty God,
that the power of the Sacrament we have received
may find growth in these your servants
and that the effects of the sacrifice we have offered
may be felt by us all.
Through Christ our Lord.

THE CONCLUSION OF THE CELEBRATION

The Conclusion of the Celebration ends the ceremony and prepares the couple to begin their lives as a married couple. After the Final Blessing, the bride, groom, and wedding party recess out of the church.

THE FINAL BLESSING

The Final Blessing, said by the deacon or priest, concludes the celebration. All options include the blessing of the sign of the cross.

OPTION 1

May God the eternal Father
keep you of one heart in love for one another,
that the peace of Christ may dwell in you
and abide always in your home.

Response: Amen.

May you be blessed in your children,
have solace in your friends
and enjoy true peace with everyone.

Response: Amen.

May you be witnesses in the world to God's charity,
so that the afflicted and needy who have known your kindness
may one day receive you thankfully
into the eternal dwelling of God.

Response: Amen.

And may almighty God bless all of you, who are gathered here,
the Father, and the Son, and the Holy Spirit.

Response: Amen.

OPTION 2

May God the all-powerful Father grant you his joy
and bless you in your children.

Response: Amen.

May the Only Begotten Son of God
stand by you with compassion in good times and in bad.

Response: Amen.

May the Holy Spirit of God
always pour forth his love into your hearts.

Response: Amen.

And may almighty God bless all of you, who are gathered here,
the Father, and the Son, and the Holy Spirit.

Response: Amen.

May the Lord Jesus,
who graced the marriage at Cana by his presence,
bless you and your loved ones.

Response: Amen.

May he, who loved the Church to the end,
unceasingly pour his love into your hearts.

Response: Amen.

May the Lord grant
that, bearing witness to faith in his Resurrection,
you may await with joy the blessed hope to come.

Response: Amen.

And may almighty God bless all of you, who are gathered here,
the Father, and the Son, and the Holy Spirit.

Response: Amen.

The Order of Celebrating Matrimony Without Mass

RITE 2

PART 1: **THE INTRODUCTORY RITE**
Welcome
Procession
Greeting
◎ The Collect

PART 2: **THE LITURGY OF THE WORD**
◎ Readings
Homily

PART 3: **THE CELEBRATION OF MATRIMONY**
The Introduction and Questions Before Consent
◎ The Consent
◎ The Reception of Consent
◎ The Blessing and Giving of Rings
◎ The Blessing and Giving of the *Arras* (Optional)
The Universal Prayer
◎ The Blessing and Placing of the *Lazo* or the Veil
(Optional)
◎ The Nuptial Blessing
◎ Holy Communion (Optional)

PART 4: **THE CONCLUSION OF THE CELEBRATION**
◎ The Final Blessing
Recessional

◎ *Indicates a step in your planning process.*

THE INTRODUCTORY RITE

The Introductory Rite begins the wedding. The priest or deacon, groom, parents, bridal party, and bride enter the church. The priest or deacon welcomes them either before they enter the church or after everyone has reached their seats and the bride and groom are standing at the altar. He then greets the congregation and begins the ceremony.

THE COLLECT

The Collect is prayed after the procession and greeting. It brings everyone together in prayer and prepares them for the liturgy.

OPTION 1

Be attentive to our prayers, O Lord,
and in your kindness
pour out your grace on these your servants N. and N.,
that, coming together before your altar,
they may be confirmed in love for one another.
Through our Lord Jesus Christ, your Son,
who lives and reigns with you in the unity of the Holy Spirit,
one God, for ever and ever.

OPTION 2

Please note: *This option may not be used if Option 1 of the Nuptial Blessing on page 49 is selected.*

O God, who consecrated the bond of Marriage
by so great a mystery
that in the wedding covenant you foreshadow
the Sacrament of Christ and his Church,

grant, we pray, to these your servants,
that what they receive in faith
they may live out in deeds.
Through our Lord Jesus Christ, your Son,
who lives and reigns with you in the unity of the Holy Spirit,
one God, for ever and ever.

OPTION 3

O God, who in creating the human race
willed that man and wife should be one,
join, we pray, in a bond of inseparable love
these your servants who are to be united in the covenant of Marriage,
so that, as you make their love fruitful,
they may become, by your grace, witnesses to charity itself.
Through our Lord Jesus Christ, your Son,
Who lives and reigns with you in the unity of the Holy Spirit,
One God, for ever and ever.

OPTION 4

Grant, we pray, almighty God,
that these your servants,
now to be joined by the Sacrament of Matrimony,
may grow in the faith they profess
and enrich your Church with faithful offspring.
Through our Lord Jesus Christ, your Son,
who lives and reigns with you in the unity of the Holy Spirit,
one God, for ever and ever.

OPTION 5

Be attentive to our prayers, O Lord,
And in your kindness uphold
what you have established for the increase of the human race,

so that the union you have created
may be kept safe by your assistance.
Through our Lord Jesus Christ, your Son,
Who lives and reigns with you in the unity of the Holy Spirit,
One God, for ever and ever.

OPTION 6

O God, who since the beginning of the world
have blessed the increase of offspring,
show favor to our supplications
and pour forth the help of your blessing
on these your servants N. and N.,
so that in the union of Marriage
they may be bound together
in mutual affection,
in likeness of mind,
and in shared holiness.
Through our Lord Jesus Christ, your Son,
who lives and reigns with you in the unity of the Holy Spirit,
one God, for ever and ever.

THE LITURGY OF THE WORD

As a couple, you will choose two or three readings, plus a Responsorial Psalm, to incorporate in your ceremony. After the readings, the priest or deacon will deliver a homily that draws from these readings in the context of the celebration of matrimony.

Below are summaries of the readings. At least one reading must explicitly reference marriage. These are marked with a *. For the full readings, see page 73.

FIRST READING

*OPTION 1 – Genesis 1:26–28, 31a: Man and woman were created for one another. This story of the creation shows the beauty and complementarity of the relationship between man and woman.

*OPTION 2 – Genesis 2:18–24: This reading celebrates the special bond between a man and woman. It is a beautiful moment when Adam sees Eve for the first time, exclaiming, "This one, at last, is bone of my bones and flesh of my flesh."

*OPTION 3 – Genesis 24: 48–51, 58–67: The story of Rebekah and Isaac's marriage celebrates marriage as a gift from God. Rebekah gives her consent and follows the will of God in marrying Isaac. This passage includes a blessing for the bride.

*OPTION 4 – Tobit 7:6–14: Sarah and Tobiah seek peace and prosperity on their marriage. After facing several obstacles, they are united as husband and wife. In times of suffering, they find joy in following God's plan.

*OPTION 5 – Tobit 8:4b–8: This reading captures a very special and intimate moment. Tobiah and Sarah begin their wedding night together in prayer. They place God at the center of their marriage and ask him to bless their life together.

*OPTION 6 – Proverbs 31:10–13, 19–20, 30–31: Finding the woman you want to spend the rest of your life with is a beautiful thing. Someone who will challenge you, serve others, and bring you closer to God.

OPTION 7 – Song of Songs 2:8–10, 14, 16a; 8:6–7a: Song of Songs is a beautiful collection of poems that reflect the intimate words of a lover. This passage voices the desire to be together and the incredible power of love.

*OPTION 8 – Sirach 26:1–4, 13–16: This reading rejoices in the joy a good wife brings to her husband through her thoughtfulness, decency, and virtue.

OPTION 9 – Jeremiah 31:31–32a, 33–34a: This reading shows the love God has for us. God instituted a new covenant in which His love became inscribed in our hearts. Similarly, the covenant of marriage will be a covenant of love between you, your spouse, and God.

Note: *If you are incorporating a First Reading and a Second Reading and your wedding is held during the Easter season, the First Reading should be from the Book of Revelation. Speak with your priest or deacon to make this selection.*

RESPONSORIAL PSALM

OPTION 1 – Psalm 33:12 and 18, 20–21, 22: "The earth is full of the goodness of the Lord."

OPTION 2 – Psalm 34:2–3, 4–5, 6–7, 8–9: "I will bless the Lord at all times." OR "Taste and see the goodness of the Lord."

OPTION 3 – Psalm 103:1–2, 8 and 13, 17–18a: "The Lord is kind and merciful." OR "The Lord's kindness is everlasting to those who fear him."

OPTION 4 – 112:1bc–2, 3–4, 5–7a, 7b–8, 9: "Blessed the man who greatly delights in the Lord's commands." OR "Alleluia."

*OPTION 5 – Psalm 128:1–2, 3, 4–5ac and 6a: "Blessed are those who fear the Lord." OR "See how the Lord blesses those who fear him."

OPTION 6 – Psalm 145:8–9, 10 and 15, 17–18: "How good is the Lord to all."

OPTION 7 – Psalm 148:1–2, 3–4, 9–10, 11–13ab, 13c–14a: "Let all praise the name of the Lord." OR "Alleluia."

SECOND READING

OPTION 1 – Romans 8:31b–35, 37–39: It is only by placing God at the center of everything that we can make sense of life. When we place something or someone else at the center of our lives we set ourselves up for a gnawing dissatisfaction.

OPTION 2 – Romans 12:1–2, 9–18 (long form) OR Romans 12:1–2, 9–13 (short form): The things of this world can distract us in a hundred different ways. But this reading encourages a more radical way of living, with love and God as the center.

OPTION 3 – Romans 15: 1b–3a, 5–7, 13: Love isn't always easy. This reading asks God to help us truly love one another, despite each other's faults.

OPTION 4 – 1 Corinthians 6:13c–15a, 17–20: This reading encourages us to remember that we were made for God, and it is in God that we will flourish.

OPTION 5 – 1 Corinthians 12:31–13:8a: St. Paul's words encourage us to persevere in love. He assures readers that when love is patient, kind, and rejoices with the truth, it endures all things.

OPTION 6 – Ephesians 4:1–6: In this reading, St. Paul encourages us to live the best life that we can, to embrace our own journey, and to bear with one another through love.

*OPTION 7 – Ephesians 5:2a, 21–33 (long form) OR Ephesians 5:2a, 25–32 (short form): Husbands are asked to lay down their entire lives for their wives, and wives are encouraged to show love and respect for their husbands.

OPTION 8 – Philippians 4:4–9: This is an invitation to rejoice, and encouragement to have no anxiety if we put God at the center of our lives. He brings us joy when we focus on whatever is true, honorable, just, pure, lovely, and gracious.

OPTION 9 – Colossians 3:12–17: This reading celebrates a life of character and virtue. It talks about the greatest virtue of love and encourages us to invite Jesus to bring peace and love into our hearts.

OPTION 10 – Hebrews 13:1–4a, 5–6b: Marriage is something worth celebrating and holding in high esteem. Marriage is at its best when both husband and wife seek help in God.

*OPTION 11 – 1 Peter 3:1–9: This reading talks about how true beauty is not found on the outside, but within. It encourages us to exercise compassion and to be a blessing for one another through our conduct.

OPTION 12 – 1 John 3:18–24: Life is full of challenges, but God will always help when we follow his commandment to love one another "in deed and truth."

OPTION 13 – 1 John 4:7–12: This passage encourages us to love one another because God loved us. We receive this gift of love from God and participate in it by loving others.

OPTION 14 – Revelation 19:1,5–9a: This reading is from the last book of the Bible. It captures John's vision of the wedding feast of the Lamb, of Jesus at the end of time. It is a beautiful way to see how marriage ultimately points us to heaven.

ALLELUIA VERSE

OPTION 1 – 1 John 4:7b: "Everyone who loves is begotten of God and knows God."

OPTION 2 – 1 John 4:8b and 11: "God is love; let us love one another, as God has loved us."

OPTION 3 – 1 John 4:12: "If we love one another, God remains in us and his love is brought to perfection in us."

OPTION 4 – 1 John 4:16: "Whoever remains in love, remains in God and God in him."

OPTION 5 – Psalm 134:3: "May the LORD bless you from Zion, he who made both heaven and earth."

GOSPEL

OPTION 1 – Matthew 5:1–12a: This passage captures Jesus' Sermon on the Mount. He gives a beautiful and powerful vision of a life well lived in the famous Beatitudes.

OPTION 2 – Matthew 5:13–16: Jesus tells his disciples they can have an incredible impact on the world and the people around them if they boldly live out their faith.

OPTION 3 – Matthew 7:21, 24–29 (long form) OR Matthew 7:21, 24–25 (short form): Jesus tells the parable of a man who built his house on rock and a man who built his house on sand. A marriage that puts God at the center is a marriage built on rock.

*OPTION 4 – Matthew 19:3–6: Marriage is forever. In this reading, Jesus is questioned about divorce, and he responds saying, "what God has joined together, man must not separate."

OPTION 5 – Matthew 22:35–40: Love is a beautiful thing. And it is our calling. When someone asks Jesus what the greatest commandment is, he replies that the greatest commandment is to love God with all your heart, soul, and mind, and the second is to love your neighbor as yourself.

*OPTION 6 – Mark 10:6–9: Jesus celebrates the beauty of the union between man and woman in marriage, and stresses that what God has joined together no one must separate.

*OPTION 7 – John 2:1–11: Jesus performs his first miracle at a wedding. His act of turning water into wine symbolizes how God gives in abundance to those who have faith and believe in his goodness.

OPTION 8 – John 15:9–12: As he prepares to leave his disciples and ascend into Heaven, Jesus tells them that the path to complete joy is to love one another as he has loved them. He encourages them (and us) to remain in his love.

OPTION 9 – John 15:12–16: There is no greater love than laying down your life for a friend. Christ laid down his life for us, demonstrating the love of God. Husbands and wives are called to love as Christ loved us by sacrificing for one another and by living selflessly.

OPTION 10 – John 17:20-26 (long form) OR John 17:20–23 (short form): Jesus desires that we will know the love of God the Father and that we will be with him in Heaven. Through your love for one another, you and your spouse will strive to bring each other closer to God and closer to Heaven.

THE CELEBRATION OF MATRIMONY

This is the part of the ceremony where the bride and groom officially become husband and wife. When prompted by the priest or deacon, the bride and groom exchange vows (called "The Exchange of Consent") and pledge their commitment to remain together for the rest of their lives.

THE INTRODUCTION AND QUESTIONS BEFORE CONSENT

After the priest or deacon addresses the couple with the following words, they declare their intentions to marry one another by separately responding to his questions:

Dearly beloved,
you have come together into the house of the Church,
so that in the presence of the Church's minister and the community
your intention to enter into Marriage
may be strengthened by the Lord with a sacred seal.
Christ abundantly blesses the love that binds you.
through a special Sacrament,
he enriches and strengthens
those he has already consecrated by Holy Baptism,
that they may be faithful to each other for ever
and assume all the responsibilities of married life.
And so, in the presence of the Church,
I ask you to state your intentions.

N. and N., have you come here to enter into Marriage
without coercion,
freely and wholeheartedly?

The bride and groom each respond: I have.

Are you prepared, as you follow the path of Marriage,
to love and honor each other
for as long as you both shall live?

The bride and groom each respond: I am.

Are you prepared to accept children lovingly from God
and to bring them up
according to the law of Christ and his Church?

The bride and groom each respond: I am

THE CONSENT

You and your fiancé will exchange marriage vows, either with full recitation
or by simply saying "I do" after the priest or deacon says the following:

Since it is your intention to enter the covenant of Holy Matrimony, join your
right hands and declare your consent before God and his Church.

OPTION 1

The groom says:
I, N., take you, N., to be my wife.
I promise to be faithful to you,
in good times and in bad,
in sickness and in health,
to love you and to honor you
all the days of my life.

The bride says:

I, N., take you, N., to be my husband.
I promise to be faithful to you,
in good times and in bad,
in sickness and in health,
to love you and to honor you
all the days of my life.

The groom says:

I, N., take you, N., for my lawful wife,
to have and to hold, from this day forward,
for better, for worse,
for richer, for poorer,
in sickness and in health,
to love and to cherish
until death do us part.

The bride says:

I, N., take you, N., for my lawful husband,
to have and to hold, from this day forward,
for better, for worse,
for richer, for poorer,
in sickness and in health,
to love and to cherish
until death do us part.

N., do you take N., to be your wife?
Do you promise to be faithful to her
in good times and in bad,
in sickness and in health,

to love her and to honor her
all the days of your life?

The groom responds: I do.

N., do you take N., to be your husband?
Do you promise to be faithful to him
in good times and in bad,
in sickness and in health,
to love him and to honor him
all the days of your life?

The bride responds: I do.

OPTION 4

N., do you take N. for your lawful wife,
to have and to hold, from this day forward,
for better, for worse,
for richer, for poorer,
in sickness and in health,
to love and to cherish
until death do you part?

The groom responds: I do.

N., do you take N. for your lawful husband,
to have and to hold, from this day forward,
for better, for worse,
for richer, for poorer,
in sickness and in health,
to love and to cherish
until death do you part?

The bride responds: I do.

THE RECEPTION OF CONSENT

The priest or deacon serves as the Church's witness of your marriage. In this prayer, the priest or deacon acknowledges the consent of the bride and groom.

OPTION 1

May the Lord in his kindness strengthen the consent
you have declared before the Church,
and graciously bring to fulfillment his blessing within you.
What God joins together, let no one put asunder.

OPTION 2

May the God of Abraham, the God of Isaac, the God of Jacob,
the God who joined together our first parents in paradise,
strengthen and bless in Christ
the consent you have declared before the Church,
so that what God joins together, no one may put asunder.

THE BLESSING AND GIVING OF RINGS

The priest or deacon says a blessing over your rings before you place them on each other's ring finger as a symbol of your marriage vows.

OPTION 1

May the Lord bless these rings,
which you will give to each other
as a sign of love and fidelity.

Bless, O Lord, these rings,
which we bless in your name,
so that those who wear them
may remain entirely faithful to each other,
abide in peace and in your will,
and live always in mutual charity.
Through Christ our Lord.

Bless and sanctify your servants
in their love, O Lord,
and let these rings, a sign of their faithfulness,
remind them of their love for one another.
Through Christ our Lord.

THE BLESSING AND GIVING OF THE *ARRAS*

If the occasion suggests, the rite of blessing and giving of the *arras* (coins) may take place after the blessing and giving of rings. Speak with your priest or deacon if you are interested in integrating this into your ceremony.

THE UNIVERSAL PRAYER

Also known as the Prayer of the Faithful, this is a collection of intercessory prayers. Your priest or deacon will have several options available for you to choose from. It may also be possible for you to craft your own Universal Prayer with the assistance of your priest or deacon.

THE BLESSING AND PLACING OF THE *LAZO* OR VEIL

According to local customs, the rite of blessing and placing of the *lazo* (wedding garland) or of the veil may take place before the Nuptial Blessing. You and your spouse remain kneeling. If the *lazo* has not been placed earlier, it may be placed at this time. Alternatively, a veil is placed over the head of the wife and the shoulders of the husband. This symbolizes the bond that unites them. Speak with your priest or deacon if you are interested in integrating this into your ceremony.

THE NUPTIAL BLESSING

The Nuptial Blessing, split into two parts with a moment of silence in between, is prayed aloud by the priest after the Lord's Prayer (the Our Father). It is a beautiful moment after the couple has exchanged vows to ask God to bless them and their marriage. If your ceremony includes the distribution of Holy Communion, it will follow the Nuptial Blessing.

Part I of The Nuptial Blessing
Words appearing in parenthesis are omitted if the bride and/or groom will not be receiving Communion.

OPTION 1

Dear brothers and sisters,
let us humbly pray to the Lord
that on these his servants, now married in Christ,
he may mercifully pour out
the blessing of his grace
and make of one heart in love
(by the Sacrament of Christ's Body and Blood)
those he has joined by a holy covenant.

Now let us humbly invoke God's blessing
upon this bride and groom,
that in his kindness he may favor with his help
those on whom he has bestowed the Sacrament of Matrimony.

Let us pray to the Lord for this bride and groom,
who come to the altar as they begin their married life,
that (partaking of the Body and Blood of Christ)
they may always be bound together by love for one another.

Part II of The Nuptial Blessing

Words appearing in parenthesis may be omitted if the bride and groom are
beyond childbearing years, or if other circumstances suggest their omission.

Please note: *This option may not be used if Option 2 of the Collect on page 33 is selected.*

O God, who by your mighty power
created all things out of nothing,
and, when you had set in place
the beginnings of the universe,
formed man and woman in your own image,
making the woman an inseparable helpmate to the man,
that they might no longer be two, but one flesh,
and taught that what you were pleased to make one
must never be divided;

O God, who consecrated the bond of Marriage
by so great a mystery
that in the wedding covenant you foreshadowed
the Sacrament of Christ and his Church;

O God, by whom woman is joined to man
and the companionship they had in the beginning
is endowed with the one blessing
not forfeited by original sin
nor washed away by the flood.

Look now with favor on these your servants,
joined together in Marriage,
who ask to be strengthened by your blessing.
Send down on them the grace of the Holy Spirit
and pour your love into their hearts,
that they may remain faithful in the Marriage covenant.

May the grace of love and peace
abide in your daughter N.,
and let her always follow the example of those holy women
whose praises are sung in the Scriptures.
May her husband entrust his heart to her,
so that, acknowledging her as his equal
and his joint heir to the life of grace,
he may show her due honor
and cherish her always
with the love that Christ has for his Church.

And now, Lord, we implore you:
may these your servants
hold fast to the faith and keep your commandments;
made one in the flesh,
may they be blameless in all they do;
and with the strength that comes from the Gospel,
may they bear true witness to Christ before all;
(may they be blessed with children,
and prove themselves virtuous parents,
who live to see their children's children).

And grant that,
reaching at last together the fullness of years
for which they hope,
they may come to the life of the blessed
in the Kingdom of Heaven.
Through Christ our Lord.

OPTION 2

Holy Father,
who formed man in your own image,
male and female you created them,
so that as husband and wife, united in body and heart,
they might fulfill their calling in the world;

O God, who, to reveal the great design you formed in your love,
willed that the love of spouses for each other
should foreshadow the covenant you graciously made with your people,
so that, by fulfillment of the sacramental sign,
the mystical marriage of Christ with his Church
might become manifest
in the union of husband and wife among your faithful;

Graciously stretch out your right hand
over these your servants (N. and N.), we pray,
and pour into their hearts the power of the Holy Spirit.

Grant, O Lord,
that, as they enter upon this sacramental union,
they may share with one another the gifts of your love
and, by being for each other a sign of your presence,
become one heart and one mind.
May they also sustain, O Lord, by their deeds
the home they are forming

(and prepare their children
to become members of your heavenly household
by raising them in the way of the Gospel).

Graciously crown with your blessings your daughter N.,
so that, by being a good wife (and mother),
she may bring warmth to her home with a love that is pure
and adorn it with welcoming graciousness.

Bestow a heavenly blessing also, O Lord,
on N., your servant,
that he may be a worthy, good and
faithful husband (and a provident father).

Grant, holy Father,
that, desiring to approach your table
as a couple joined in Marriage in your presence,
they may one day have the joy
of taking part in your great banquet in heaven.
Through Christ our Lord.

OPTION 3

Holy Father, maker of the whole world,
who created man and woman in your own image
and willed that their union be crowned with your blessing,
we humbly beseech you for these your servants,
who are joined today in the Sacrament of Matrimony.

May your abundant blessing, Lord,
come down upon this bride, N.,
and upon N., her companion for life,
and may the power of your Holy Spirit
set their hearts aflame from on high,

so that, living out together the gift of Matrimony,
they may (adorn their family with children
and) enrich the Church.

In happiness may they praise you, O Lord,
in sorrow may they seek you out;
may they have the joy of your presence
to assist them in their toil,
and know that you are near
to comfort them in their need;
let them pray to you in the holy assembly
and bear witness to you in the world,
and after a happy old age,
together with the circle of friends that surrounds them,
may they come to the Kingdom of Heaven.
Through Christ our Lord.

HOLY COMMUNION (OPTIONAL)

If you would like to have Communion distributed during your ceremony,
the priest or deacon will do so at this time.

THE CONCLUSION OF THE CELEBRATION

The Conclusion of the Celebration ends the ceremony and prepares the couple to begin their lives as a married couple. After the Final Blessing, the bride, groom, and wedding party recess out of the church.

THE FINAL BLESSING

The Final Blessing, said by the deacon or priest, concludes the celebration. All options include the blessing of the sign of the cross.

OPTION 1

May God the eternal Father
keep you of one heart in love for one another,
that the peace of Christ may dwell in you
and abide always in your home.

Response: Amen.

May you be blessed in your children,
have solace in your friends
and enjoy true peace with everyone.

Response: Amen.

May you be witnesses in the world to God's charity,
so that the afflicted and needy who have known your kindness

may one day receive you thankfully
into the eternal dwelling of God.

Response: Amen.

And may almighty God bless all of you, who are gathered here,
the Father, and the Son, and the Holy Spirit.

Response: Amen.

OPTION 2

May God the all-powerful Father grant you his joy
and bless you in your children.

Response: Amen.

May the Only Begotten Son of God
stand by you with compassion in good times and in bad.

Response: Amen.

May the Holy Spirit of God
always pour forth his love into your hearts.

Response: Amen.

And may almighty God bless all of you, who are gathered here,
the Father, and the Son, and the Holy Spirit.

Response: Amen.

May the Lord Jesus,
who graced the marriage at Cana by his presence,
bless you and your loved ones.

Response: Amen.

May he, who loved the Church to the end,
unceasingly pour his love into your hearts.

Response: Amen.

May the Lord grant
that, bearing witness to faith in his Resurrection,
you may await with joy the blessed hope to come.

Response: Amen.

And may almighty God bless all of you, who are gathered here,
the Father, and the Son, and the Holy Spirit.

Response: Amen.

The Order of Celebrating Matrimony Between a Catholic and Catechumen or a Non-Christian

RITE 3

PART 1:   **THE RITE OF RECEPTION**
Welcome
Procession
Greeting

PART 2:   **THE LITURGY OF THE WORD**
◎ Readings
Homily

PART 3:   **THE CELEBRATION OF MATRIMONY**
The Introduction and Questions Before Consent
◎ The Consent
◎ The Reception of Consent
◎ The Blessing and Giving of Rings
◎ The Blessing and Giving of the *Arras* (Optional)
The Universal Prayer
◎ The Blessing Placing of the *Lazo* or the *Veil*
(Optional)
The Nuptial Blessing

PART 4:   **THE CONCLUSION OF THE CELEBRATION**
The Final Blessing
Recessional

◎ *Indicates a step in your planning process.*

THE RITE OF RECEPTION

The Rite of Reception begins the wedding. The priest or deacon, groom, parents, bridal party, and bride enter the church. The priest or deacon welcomes them either before they enter the church or after everyone has reached their seats and the bride and groom are standing at the altar. He then greets all those who have gathered to celebrate the couple's marriage, and begins the liturgy.

THE LITURGY OF THE WORD

As a couple, you will choose one or two readings to incorporate in your ceremony. After the readings, the priest or deacon will deliver a homily that draws from these readings in the context of the celebration of matrimony.

Below are summaries of the readings. At least one reading must explicitly reference marriage. These are marked with a *. For the full readings, see page 73.

FIRST READING

*OPTION 1 – Genesis 1:26–28, 31a: Man and woman were created for one another. This story of the creation shows the beauty and complementarity of the relationship between man and woman.

*OPTION 2 – Genesis 2:18–24: This reading celebrates the special bond between a man and woman. It is a beautiful moment when Adam sees Eve for the first time, exclaiming, "This one, at last, is bone of my bones and flesh of my flesh."

*OPTION 3 – Genesis 24: 48–51, 58–67: The story of Rebekah and Isaac's marriage celebrates marriage as a gift from God. Rebekah gives her consent and follows the will of God in marrying Isaac. This passage includes a blessing for the bride.

*OPTION 4 – Tobit 7:6–14: Sarah and Tobiah seek peace and prosperity on their marriage. After facing several obstacles, they are united as husband and wife. In times of suffering, they find joy in following God's plan.

*OPTION 5 – Tobit 8:4b–8: This reading captures a very special and intimate moment. Tobiah and Sarah begin their wedding night together in prayer. They place God at the center of their marriage and ask him to bless their life together.

*OPTION 6 – Proverbs 31:10–13, 19–20, 30–31: Finding the woman you want to spend the rest of your life with is a beautiful thing. Someone who will challenge you, serve others, and bring you closer to God.

OPTION 7 – Song of Songs 2:8–10, 14, 16a; 8:6–7a: Song of Songs is a beautiful collection of poems that reflect the intimate words of a lover. This passage voices the desire to be together and the incredible power of love.

*OPTION 8 – Sirach 26:1–4, 13–16: This reading rejoices in the joy a good wife brings to her husband through her thoughtfulness, decency, and virtue.

OPTION 9 – Jeremiah 31:31–32a, 33–34a: This reading shows the love God has for us. God instituted a new covenant in which His love became inscribed in our hearts. Similarly, the covenant of marriage will be a covenant of love between you, your spouse, and God.

RESPONSORIAL PSALM

OPTION 1 – Psalm 33:12 and 18, 20–21, 22: "The earth is full of the goodness of the Lord."

OPTION 2 – Psalm 34:2–3, 4–5, 6–7, 8–9: "I will bless the Lord at all times." OR "Taste and see the goodness of the Lord."

OPTION 3 – Psalm 103:1–2, 8 and 13, 17–18a: "The Lord is kind and merciful." OR "The Lord's kindness is everlasting to those who fear him."

OPTION 4 – 112:1bc–2, 3–4, 5–7a, 7b–8, 9: "Blessed the man who greatly delights in the Lord's commands." OR "Alleluia."

*OPTION 5 – Psalm 128:1–2, 3, 4–5ac and 6a: "Blessed are those who fear the Lord." OR "See how the Lord blesses those who fear him."

OPTION 6 – Psalm 145:8–9, 10 and 15, 17–18: "How good is the Lord to all."

OPTION 7 – Psalm 148:1–2, 3–4, 9–10, 11–13ab, 13c–14a: "Let all praise the name of the Lord." OR "Alleluia."

SECOND READING

OPTION 1 – Romans 8:31b–35, 37–39: It is only by placing God at the center of everything that we can make sense of life. When we place something or someone else at the center of our lives we set ourselves up for a gnawing dissatisfaction.

OPTION 2 – Romans 12:1–2, 9–18 (long form) OR Romans 12:1–2, 9–13 (short form): The things of this world can distract us in a hundred different ways. But this reading encourages a more radical way of living, with love and God as the center.

OPTION 3 – Romans 15: 1b–3a, 5–7, 13: Love isn't always easy. This reading asks God to help us truly love one another, despite each other's faults.

OPTION 4 – 1 Corinthians 6:13c–15a, 17–20: This reading encourages us to remember that we were made for God, and it is in God that we will flourish.

OPTION 5 – 1 Corinthians 12:31–13:8a: St. Paul's words encourage us to persevere in love. He assures readers that when love is patient, kind, and rejoices with the truth, it endures all things.

OPTION 6 – Ephesians 4:1–6: In this reading, St. Paul encourages us to live the best life that we can, to embrace our own journey, and to bear with one another through love.

*OPTION 7 – Ephesians 5:2a, 21–33 (long form) OR Ephesians 5:2a, 25–32 (short form): Husbands are asked to lay down their entire lives for their wives, and wives are encouraged to show love and respect for their husbands.

OPTION 8 – Philippians 4:4–9: This is an invitation to rejoice, and encouragement to have no anxiety if we put God at the center of our lives. He brings us joy when we focus on whatever is true, honorable, just, pure, lovely, and gracious.

OPTION 9 – Colossians 3:12–17: This reading celebrates a life of character and virtue. It talks about the greatest virtue of love and encourages us to invite Jesus to bring peace and love into our hearts.

OPTION 10 – Hebrews 13:1–4a, 5–6b: Marriage is something worth celebrating and holding in high esteem. Marriage is at its best when both husband and wife seek help in God.

*OPTION 11 – 1 Peter 3:1–9: This reading talks about how true beauty is not found on the outside, but within. It encourages us to exercise compassion and to be a blessing for one another through our conduct.

OPTION 12 – 1 John 3:18–24: Life is full of challenges, but God will always help when we follow his commandment to love one another "in deed and truth."

OPTION 13 – 1 John 4:7–12: This passage encourages us to love one another because God loved us. We receive this gift of love from God and participate in it by loving others.

OPTION 14 – Revelation 19:1,5–9a: This reading is from the last book of the Bible. It captures John's vision of the wedding feast of the Lamb, of Jesus at the end of time. It is a beautiful way to see how marriage ultimately points us to heaven.

GOSPEL

OPTION 1 – Matthew 5:1–12a: This passage captures Jesus' Sermon on the Mount. He gives a beautiful and powerful vision of a life well lived in the famous Beatitudes.

OPTION 2 – Matthew 5:13–16: Jesus tells his disciples they can have an incredible impact on the world and the people around them if they boldly live out their faith.

OPTION 3 – Matthew 7:21, 24–29 (long form) OR Matthew 7:21, 24–25 (short form): Jesus tells the parable of a man who built his house on rock and a man who built his house on sand. A marriage that puts God at the center is a marriage built on rock.

*OPTION 4 – Matthew 19:3–6: Marriage is forever. In this reading, Jesus is questioned about divorce, and he responds saying, "what God has joined together, man must not separate."

OPTION 5 – Matthew 22:35–40: Love is a beautiful thing. And it is our calling. When someone asks Jesus what the greatest commandment is, he replies that the greatest commandment is to love God with all your heart, soul, and mind, and the second is to love your neighbor as yourself.

*OPTION 6 – Mark 10:6–9: Jesus celebrates the beauty of the union between man and woman in marriage, and stresses that what God has joined together no one must separate.

*OPTION 7 – John 2:1–11: Jesus performs his first miracle at a wedding. His act of turning water into wine symbolizes how God gives in abundance to those who have faith and believe in his goodness.

OPTION 8 – John 15:9–12: As he prepares to leave his disciples and ascend into Heaven, Jesus tells them that the path to complete joy is to love one another as he has loved them. He encourages them (and us) to remain in his love.

OPTION 9 – John 15:12–16: There is no greater love than laying down your life for a friend. Christ laid down his life for us, demonstrating the love of God. Husbands and wives are called to love as Christ loved us by sacrificing for one another and by living selflessly.

OPTION 10 – John 17:20-26 (long form) OR John 17:20–23 (short form): Jesus desires that we will know the love of God the Father and that we will be with him in Heaven. Through your love for one another, you and your spouse will strive to bring each other closer to God and closer to Heaven.

THE CELEBRATION OF MATRIMONY

This is the part of the ceremony where the bride and groom officially become husband and wife. When prompted by the priest or deacon, the bride and groom exchange vows (called "The Exchange of Consent") and pledge their commitment to remain together for the rest of their lives.

————————————

THE INTRODUCTION AND QUESTIONS BEFORE CONSENT

After the priest or deacon addresses the couple with the following words, they declare their intentions to marry one another by responding to his questions one at a time:

Dearly beloved,
you have come together here
Before a minister of the Church
and in the presence of the community
So that your intention to enter into Marriage
may be strengthened by the Lord with a sacred seal.
and your love be enriched with his blessing,
so that you may have strength
to be faithful to each other for ever
and to assume all the responsibilities of married life.
And so, in the presence of the Church,
I ask you to state your intentions.

N. and N., have you come here to enter into Marriage
without coercion,
freely and wholeheartedly?

The bride and groom each respond: I have.

Are you prepared, as you follow the path of Marriage,
to love and honor each other
for as long as you both shall live?

The bride and groom each respond: I am.

Are you prepared to accept children lovingly from God
and to bring them up
according to the law of Christ and his Church?

The bride and groom each respond: I am.

THE CONSENT

You and your fiancé will exchange marriage vows, either with full recitation
or by simply saying "I do" after the priest or deacon says the following:

Since it is your intention to enter the covenant of Holy Matrimony, join your
right hands and declare your consent before God and his Church.

OPTION 1

The groom says:
I, N., take you, N., to be my wife.
I promise to be faithful to you,
in good times and in bad,
in sickness and in health,
to love you and to honor you
all the days of my life.

The bride says:
I, N., take you, N., to be my husband.
I promise to be faithful to you,

in good times and in bad,
in sickness and in health,
to love you and to honor you
all the days of my life.

OPTION 2

The groom says:
I, N., take you, N., for my lawful wife,
to have and to hold, from this day forward,
for better, for worse,
for richer, for poorer,
in sickness and in health,
to love and to cherish
until death do us part.

The bride says:
I, N., take you, N., for my lawful husband,
to have and to hold, from this day forward,
for better, for worse,
for richer, for poorer,
in sickness and in health,
to love and to cherish
until death do us part.

OPTION 3

N., do you take N., to be your wife?
Do you promise to be faithful to her
in good times and in bad,
in sickness and in health,
to love her and to honor her
all the days of your life?

The groom responds: I do.

N., do you take N., to be your husband?
Do you promise to be faithful to him
in good times and in bad,
in sickness and in health,
to love him and to honor him
all the days of your life?

The bride responds: I do.

OPTION 4

N., do you take N. for your lawful wife,
to have and to hold, from this day forward,
for better, for worse,
for richer, for poorer,
in sickness and in health,
to love and to cherish
until death do you part?

The groom responds: I do.

N., do you take N. for your lawful husband,
to have and to hold, from this day forward,
for better, for worse,
for richer, for poorer,
in sickness and in health,
to love and to cherish
until death do you part?

The bride responds: I do.

THE RECEPTION OF CONSENT

The priest or deacon serves as the Church's witness of your marriage. In this prayer, the priest or deacon acknowledges the consent of the bride and groom.

OPTION 1

May the Lord in his kindness strengthen the consent
you have declared before the Church,
and graciously bring to fulfillment his blessing within you.
What God joins together, let no one put asunder.

OPTION 2

May the God of Abraham, the God of Isaac, the God of Jacob,
the God who joined together our first parents in paradise,
strengthen and bless in Christ
the consent you have declared before the Church,
so that what God joins together, no one may put asunder.

THE BLESSING AND GIVING OF RINGS

The priest or deacon says a blessing over your rings before you place them on each other's ring finger as a symbol of your marriage vows.

OPTION 1

May the Lord bless these rings,
which you will give to each other
as a sign of love and fidelity.

OPTION 2

Bless, O Lord, these rings,
which we bless in your name,
so that those who wear them
may remain entirely faithful to each other,
abide in peace and in your will,
and live always in mutual charity.
Through Christ our Lord.

OPTION 3

Bless and sanctify your servants
in their love, O Lord,
and let these rings, a sign of their faithfulness,
remind them of their love for one another.
Through Christ our Lord.

THE BLESSING AND GIVING OF THE *ARRAS*

If the occasion suggests, the rite of blessing and giving of the *arras* (coins)
may take place after the blessing and giving of rings. Speak with your priest
or deacon if you are interested in integrating this into your ceremony.

THE UNIVERSAL PRAYER

Also known as the Prayer of the Faithful, this is a collection of intercessory
prayers. Your priest or deacon will have several options available for you
to choose from. It may also be possible for you to craft your own Universal
Prayer with the assistance of your priest or deacon.

THE BLESSING AND PLACING OF THE *LAZO* OR VEIL

According to local customs, the rite of blessing and placing of the *lazo* (wedding garland) or of the veil may take place before the Nuptial Blessing. You and your spouse remain kneeling. If the *lazo* has not been placed earlier, it may be placed at this time. Alternatively, a veil is placed over the head of the wife and the shoulders of the husband. This symbolizes the bond that unites them. Speak with your priest or deacon if you are interested in integrating this into your ceremony.

THE NUPTIAL BLESSING

The Nuptial Blessing, split into two parts with a moment of silence in between, is prayed aloud by the priest after the Lord's Prayer (the Our Father). It is a beautiful moment after the couple has exchanged vows to ask God to bless them and their marriage. Parts I and II of the Nuptial Blessing are pre-set for this rite.

Part I of The Nuptial Blessing
After the Lord's Prayer, the priest or deacon will extend his hands over you and say:

Now let us humbly invoke God's blessing
upon this bride and groom,
that in his kindness he may favor with his help
those on whom he has bestowed the bond of Marriage.

Part II of The Nuptial Blessing
Words appearing in parenthesis may be omitted if the bride and groom are beyond childbearing years, or if other circumstances suggest their omission.

Holy Father, maker of the whole world,
who created man and woman in your own image

and willed that their union be crowned with your blessing,
we humbly beseech you for these your servants,
who are joined today in the Marriage Covenant.
May your abundant blessing, Lord,
come down upon this bride, N.,
and upon N., her companion for life,
and may the power of your Holy Spirit
set their hearts aflame from on high,
so that, living out together the gift of Matrimony,
they may be known for the integrity of their conduct
(and be recognized as virtuous parents).

In happiness may they praise you, O Lord,
in sorrow may they seek you out;
may they have the joy of your presence
to assist them in their toil,
and know that you are near
to comfort them in their need;
and after a happy old age,
together with the circle of friends that surrounds them,
may they come to the Kingdom of Heaven.
Through Christ our Lord.

THE CONCLUSION OF THE CELEBRATION

The Conclusion of the Celebration ends the ceremony and prepares the couple to begin their lives as a married couple. The priest or deacon blesses the bride, groom, and the congregation with the sign of the cross. Afterwards, the bride, groom, and wedding party recess out of the church.

Readings

FIRST READING

The First Reading is typically from the Old Testament, which points us towards Christ and his fulfillment of God's promises.

*OPTION 1: Genesis 1:26-28, 31a
Man and woman were created for one another. This story of the creation shows the beauty and complementarity of the relationship between man and woman.

Then God said:
"Let us make man in our image, after our likeness.
Let them have dominion over the fish of the sea,
   the birds of the air, and the cattle,
   and over all the wild animals
   and all the creatures that crawl on the ground."

God created man in his image;
   in the image of God he created him;
   male and female he created them.

God blessed them, saying:
   "Be fertile and multiply;
   fill the earth and subdue it.
Have dominion over the fish of the sea, the birds of the air,
   and all the living things that move on the earth."
God looked at everything he had made, and he found it very good.

*OPTION 2: Genesis 2:18-24
This reading celebrates the special bond between a man and woman. It is a beautiful moment when Adam sees Eve for the first time, exclaiming, "This one, at last, is bone of my bones and flesh of my flesh."

The LORD God said: "It is not good for the man to be alone.
I will make a suitable partner for him."
So the LORD God formed out of the ground
  various wild animals and various birds of the air,
    and he brought them to the man to see what he would call them;
    whatever the man called each of them would be its name.
The man gave names to all the cattle,
  all the birds of the air, and all wild animals;
  but none proved to be the suitable partner for the man.

So the LORD God cast a deep sleep on the man,
  and while he was asleep,
  he took out one of his ribs and closed up its place with flesh.
The LORD God then built up into a woman the rib
  that he had taken from the man.
When he brought her to the man, the man said:

  "This one, at last, is bone of my bones
    and flesh of my flesh;
  This one shall be called 'woman,'
    for out of 'her man' this one has been taken."

That is why a man leaves his father and mother
  and clings to his wife,
  and the two of them become one body.

*OPTION 3: Genesis 24: 48-51, 58-67
*The story of Rebekah and Isaac's marriage celebrates marriage as a gift from
God. Rebekah gives her consent and follows the will of God in marrying
Isaac. This passage includes a blessing for the bride.*

The servant of Abraham said to Laban:
"I bowed down in worship to the LORD,
  blessing the LORD, the God of my master Abraham,

who had led me on the right road
to obtain the daughter of my master's kinsman for his son.
If, therefore, you have in mind to show true loyalty to my master,
let me know;
but if not, let me know that, too.
I can then proceed accordingly."

Laban and his household said in reply:
"This thing comes from the LORD;
we can say nothing to you either for or against it.
Here is Rebekah, ready for you;
take her with you,
that she may become the wife of your master's son,
as the LORD has said."

So they called Rebekah and asked her,
"Do you wish to go with this man?"
She answered, "I do."
At this they allowed their sister Rebekah and her nurse to take leave,
along with Abraham's servant and his men.
Invoking a blessing on Rebekah, they said:

"Sister, may you grow
into thousands of myriads;
And may your descendants gain possession
of the gates of their enemies!"

Then Rebekah and her maids started out;
they mounted their camels and followed the man.
so the servant took Rebekah and went on his way.

Meanwhile Isaac had gone from Beer-lahai-roi
and was living in the region of the Negeb.
One day toward evening he went out . . . in the field,

and as he looked around, he noticed that camels were approaching.
Rebekah, too, was looking about, and when she saw him,
   she alighted from her camel and asked the servant,
"Who is the man out there, walking through the fields toward us?"
"That is my master," replied the servant.
Then she covered herself with her veil.

The servant recounted to Isaac all the things he had done.
Then Isaac took Rebekah into his tent;
   he married her, and thus she became his wife.
In his love for her Isaac found solace
   after the death of his mother Sarah.

*OPTION 4: Tobit 7:6-14
Sarah and Tobiah seek peace and prosperity on their marriage. After facing several obstacles, they are united as husband and wife. In times of suffering, they find joy in following God's plan.

Raphael and Tobiah entered the house of Raguel and greeted him.
Raguel sprang up and kissed Tobiah, shedding tears of joy.
But when he heard that Tobit had lost his eyesight,
   he was grieved and wept aloud.
He said to Tobiah:
   "My child, God bless you!
You are the son of a noble and good father.
But what a terrible misfortune
   that such a righteous and charitable man
   should be afflicted with blindness!"
He continued to weep in the arms of his kinsman Tobiah.
His wife Edna also wept for Tobit;
   and even their daughter Sarah began to weep.

Afterward, Raguel slaughtered a ram from the flock
   and gave them a cordial reception.

When they had bathed and reclined to eat,
   Tobiah said to Raphael, "Brother Azariah,
   ask Raguel to let me marry my kinswoman Sarah."
Raguel overheard the words;
   so he said to the boy:
   "Eat and drink and be merry tonight,
   for no man is more entitled to marry my daughter Sarah
   than you, brother.
Besides, not even I have the right to give her to anyone but you,
   because you are my closest relative.
But I will explain the situation to you very frankly.
I have given her in marriage to seven men,
   all of whom were kinsmen of ours,
   and all died on the very night they approached her.
But now, son, eat and drink.
   I am sure the Lord will look after you both."
Tobiah answered, "I will eat or drink nothing
   until you set aside what belongs to me."

Raguel said to him: "I will do it.
She is yours according to the decree of the Book of Moses.
Your marriage to her has been decided in heaven!
Take your kinswoman
   from now on you are her love,
   and she is your beloved.
She is yours today and ever after.
And tonight, son, may the Lord of heaven prosper you both.
May he grant you mercy and peace."
Then Raguel called his daughter Sarah, and she came to him.
He took her by the hand and gave her to Tobiah with the words:
   "Take her according to the law.
According to the decree written in the Book of Moses she is your wife.
Take her and bring her back safely to your father.
And may the God of heaven grant both of you peace and prosperity."

He then called her mother and told her to bring a scroll,
  so that he might draw up a marriage contract
  stating that he gave Sarah to Tobiah as his wife
  according to the decree of the Mosaic law.
Her mother brought the scroll,
  and he drew up the contract,
  to which they affixed their seal.

Afterward they began to eat and drink.

*OPTION 5: Tobit 8:4b-8
This reading captures a very special and intimate moment. Tobiah and Sarah
begin their wedding night together in prayer. They place God at the center
of their marriage and ask him to bless their life together.

On their wedding night Tobiah arose from bed and said to his wife,
  "Sister, get up. Let us pray and beg our Lord
  to have mercy on us and to grant us deliverance."
Sarah got up, and they started to pray
  and beg that deliverance might be theirs.
They began with these words:

  "Blessed are you, O God of our fathers;
    praised be your name forever and ever.
  Let the heavens and all your creation
    praise you forever.
  You made Adam and you gave him his wife Eve
    to be his help and support;
    and from these two the human race descended.
  You said, 'It is not good for the man to be alone;
    let us make him a partner like himself.'
  Now, Lord, you know that I take this wife of mine
    not because of lust,
    but for a noble purpose.

Call down your mercy on me and on her,
   and allow us to live together to a happy old age."

They said together, "Amen, amen."

*OPTION 6: Proverbs 31:10-13, 19-20, 30-31
*Finding the woman you want to spend the rest of your life with is a beautiful
thing. This passage celebrates finding someone who will challenge you, serve
others, and bring you closer to God.*

When one finds a worthy wife,
   her value is far beyond pearls.
Her husband, entrusting his heart to her,
   has an unfailing prize.
She brings him good, and not evil,
   all the days of her life.
She obtains wool and flax
   and makes cloth with skillful hands.
She puts her hands to the distaff,
   and her fingers ply the spindle.
She reaches out her hands to the poor,
   and extends her arms to the needy.
Charm is deceptive and beauty fleeting;
   the woman who fears the LORD is to be praised.
Give her a reward of her labors,
   and let her works praise her at the city gates.

OPTION 7: Song of Songs 2:8-10, 14, 16a; 8:6-7a
*Song of Songs is a beautiful collection of poems that reflect the intimate
words of a lover. This passage voices the desire to be together and the
incredible power of love.*

Hark! my lover–here he comes
   springing across the mountains,

leaping across the hills.
My lover is like a gazelle
  or a young stag.
Here he stands behind our wall,
  gazing through the windows,
  peering through the lattices.
My lover speaks; he says to me,
  "Arise, my beloved, my dove, my beautiful one, and come!

"O my dove in the clefts of the rock,
  in the secret recesses of the cliff,
Let me see you,
  let me hear your voice,
For your voice is sweet,
  and you are lovely."

My lover belongs to me and I to him.
  He says to me:

"Set me as a seal on your heart,
  as a seal on your arm;
For stern as death is love,
  relentless as the nether world is devotion;
  its flames are a blazing fire.
Deep waters cannot quench love,
  nor floods sweep it away."

*OPTION 8: Sirach 26:1-4, 13-16
This reading rejoices in the joy a good wife brings to her husband through her thoughtfulness, decency, and virtue.

Blessed the husband of a good wife,
  twice-lengthened are his days;
A worthy wife brings joy to her husband,
  peaceful and full is his life.

A good wife is a generous gift
   bestowed upon him who fears the LORD;
Be he rich or poor, his heart is content,
   and a smile is ever on his face.

A gracious wife delights her husband,
   her thoughtfulness puts flesh on his bones;
A gift from the LORD is her governed speech,
   and her firm virtue is of surpassing worth.
Choicest of blessings is a modest wife,
   priceless her chaste soul.
A holy and decent woman adds grace upon grace;
   indeed, no price is worthy of her temperate soul.
Like the sun rising in the LORD's heavens,
   the beauty of a virtuous wife is the radiance of her home.

OPTION 9: Jeremiah 31:31-32a, 33-34a
*This reading shows the love God has for us. God instituted a new covenant
in which His love became inscribed in our hearts. Similarly, the covenant of
marriage will be a covenant of love between you, your spouse, and God.*

The days are coming, says the LORD,
   when I will make a new covenant with the house of Israel
   and the house of Judah.
It will not be like the covenant I made with their fathers:
   the day I took them by the hand
   to lead them forth from the land of Egypt.
But this is the covenant which I will make
   with the house of Israel after those days, says the LORD.
I will place my law within them, and write it upon their hearts;
   I will be their God, and they shall be my people.
No longer will they have need to teach their friends and relatives
   how to know the LORD.
All, from least to greatest, shall know me, says the LORD.

RESPONSORIAL PSALM

Originally written as songs, the Responsorial Psalm can be sung if you have a cantor. Alternately, they can be read.

OPTION 1: Psalm 33:12 and 18, 20-21,22

R. (5b) The earth is full of the goodness of the Lord.

Blessed the nation whose God is the LORD,
  the people he has chosen as his heritage.
Yes, the LORD's eyes are upon those who fear him,
  who hope in his merciful love. R

Our soul is waiting for the LORD,
  He is our help and our shield.
In him do our hearts find joy.
  We trust in his holy name. R

May your merciful love be upon us,
  as we hope in you, O LORD. R

OPTION 2: Psalm 34:2-3, 4-5, 6-7, 8-9

R. (2a) I will bless the Lord at all times.
OR:
R. (9a) Taste and see the goodness of the Lord.

I will bless the LORD at all times;
  praise of him is always in my mouth.
In the LORD my soul shall makes its boast;
  the humble shall hear and be glad. R

Glorify the LORD with me,
  together let us praise his name.
I sought the LORD, and he answered me
  from all my terrors he set me free. R

Look toward him and be radiant;
  let your faces not be abashed.
This lowly one called; the LORD heard,
  and rescued him from all his distress. R

The angel of the LORD is encamped
  around those who fear him, to rescue them.
Taste and see that the LORD is good.
  Blessed the man who seeks refuge in him. R

OPTION 3: Psalm 103:1-2, 8 and 13, 17-18a

R. (8a) The Lord is kind and merciful.
OR:
R. (see 17) The Lord's kindness is everlasting to those who fear him.

Bless the LORD, O my soul;
  and all within me, his holy name.
Bless the LORD, O my soul,
  and never forget all his benefits. R

The LORD is compassionate and gracious,
  slow to anger and rich in mercy.
As a father has compassion on his children,
  the LORD's compassion is on those who fear him. R

But the mercy of the LORD is everlasting
  upon those who hold him in fear,

upon children's children his righteousness,
    for those who keep his covenant. R

OPTION 4: 112:1bc-2, 3-4, 5-7a, 7b-8, 9

R. (cf. 1) Blessed the man who greatly delights in the Lord's commands.
OR:
R. Alleluia.

Blessed the man who fears the LORD,
    who takes great delight in his commandments.
His descendants shall be powerful on earth;
    the generation of the upright will be blest. R

Riches and wealth are in his house;
    his righteousness stands firm forever.
A light rises in the darkness for the upright;
    he is generous, merciful, and righteous. R

It goes well for the man who deals generously and lends,
    who conducts his affairs with justice.
He will never be moved;
    forever shall the righteous be remembered.
He has no fear of evil news. R

With a firm heart, he trusts in the LORD.
With a steadfast heart he will not fear;
    he will see the downfall of his foes. R

Open-handed, he gives to the poor;
    his righteousness stands firm forever.
    His might shall be exalted in glory. R

*OPTION 5: Psalm 128:1-2, 3, 4-5ac and 6a

R. (cf. 1) Blessed are those who fear the Lord.
OR:
R. (4) See how the Lord blesses those who fear him.

Blessed are all who fear the LORD,
  and walk in his ways!
By the labor of your hands you shall eat.
  You will be blessed and prosper. R

Your wife like a fruitful vine
  in the heart of your house;
Your children like shoots of the olive.
  around your table. R

Indeed thus shall be blessed
  the man who fears the LORD.
May the LORD bless you from Zion:
  all the days of your life!
  May you see your children's children. R

OPTION 6: Psalm 145:8-9, 10 and 15, 17-18

R. (9a) How good is the Lord to all.

The LORD is kind and full of compassion,
  slow to anger, abounding in mercy.
How good is the LORD to all,
  compassionate to all his creatures. R

All your works shall thank you, O LORD,
  and all your faithful ones bless you.
The eyes of all look to you
  and you give them their food in due season. R

The LORD is righteous in all his ways
  and holy in all his deeds.
The LORD is close to all who call him,
  who call on him in truth. R

OPTION 7: Psalm 148:1-2. 3-4, 9-10, 11-13ab, 13c-14a

R. (13a) Let all praise the name of the Lord.
OR:
R. Alleluia.

Praise the LORD from the heavens,
  praise him in the heights;
Praise him, all his angels,
  praise him, all his hosts. R

Praise him, sun and moon;
  praise him, all shining stars.
Praise him, highest heavens,
  and the waters above the heavens. R

Mountains and all hills,
  fruit trees and all cedars;
beasts, both wild and tame,
  creeping things and birds on the wing. R

Kings of the earth and all peoples,
  princes and all judges of the earth,
young men and maidens as well,
  the old and the young together.
Let them praise the name of the LORD,
  for his name alone is exalted. R

His splendor above heaven and earth.
  He exalts the strength of his people. R

SECOND READING

The Second Reading, also called the New Testament reading, is from one of the letters written by St. Paul or one of the Apostles. These letters speak to how we can follow Jesus and his teachings.

OPTION 1: Romans 8:31b-35, 37-39
It is only by placing God at the center of everything that we can make sense of life. When we place something or someone else at the center of our lives we set ourselves up for a gnawing dissatisfaction.

Brothers and sisters:
If God is for us, who can be against us?
He did not spare his own Son
  but handed him over for us all,
  how will he not also give us everything else along with him?
Who will bring a charge against God's chosen ones?
It is God who acquits us.
Who will condemn?
It is Christ Jesus who died, rather, was raised,
  who also is at the right hand of God,
  who indeed intercedes for us.
What will separate us from the love of Christ?
Will anguish, or distress, or persecution, or famine,
  or nakedness, or peril, or the sword?
No, in all these things, we conquer overwhelmingly
  through him who loved us.
For I am convinced that neither death, nor life,
  nor angels, nor principalities,
  nor present things, nor future things,
  nor powers, nor height, nor depth,
  nor any other creature will be able to separate us
  from the love of God in Christ Jesus our Lord.

OPTION 2: Romans 12:1-2, 9-18 (long form) OR Romans 12:1-2, 9-13 (short form)
The things of this world can distract us in a hundred different ways. But this reading encourages a more radical way of living, with love and God as the center.

I urge you, brothers and sisters, by the mercies of God,
  to offer your bodies as a living sacrifice,
  holy and pleasing to God, your spiritual worship.
Do not conform yourselves to this age
  but be transformed by the renewal of your mind,
  that you may discern what is the will of God,
  what is good and pleasing and perfect.

Let love be sincere;
  hate what is evil,
  hold on to what is good;
  love one another with mutual affection;
  anticipate one another in showing honor.
Do not grow slack in zeal,
  be fervent in spirit,
  serve the Lord.
Rejoice in hope,
  endure in affliction,
  persevere in prayer.
Contribute to the needs of the holy ones,
  exercise hospitality.
Bless those who persecute you,
  bless and do not curse them.
Rejoice with those who rejoice,
  weep with those who weep.
Have the same regard for one another;
  do not be haughty but associate with the lowly;
  do not be wise in your own estimation.

Do not repay anyone evil for evil;
  be concerned for what is noble in the sight of all.
If possible, on your part, live at peace with all.

OR

I urge you, brothers and sisters, by the mercies of God,
  to offer your bodies as a living sacrifice,
  holy and pleasing to God, your spiritual worship.
Do not conform yourselves to this age
  but be transformed by the renewal of your mind,
  that you may discern what is the will of God,
  what is good and pleasing and perfect.

Let love be sincere;
  hate what is evil,
  hold on to what is good;
  love one another with mutual affection;
  anticipate one another in showing honor.
Do not grow slack in zeal,
  be fervent in spirit,
  serve the Lord.
Rejoice in hope,
  endure in affliction,
  persevere in prayer.
Contribute to the needs of the holy ones,
  exercise hospitality.

OPTION 3: Romans 15: 1b-3a, 5-7, 13
Love isn't always easy. This reading asks God to help us truly love one another, despite each other's faults.

Brothers and sisters:
We ought to put up with the failings of the weak and not to please ourselves;

let each of us please our neighbor for the good,
   for building up.
For Christ did not please himself.
May the God of endurance and encouragement
   grant you to think in harmony with one another,
   in keeping with Christ Jesus,
   that with one accord you may with one voice
   glorify the God and Father of our Lord Jesus Christ.

Welcome one another, then, as Christ welcomed you,
   for the glory of God.
May the God of hope fill you with all joy and peace in believing,
   so that you may abound in hope by the power of the Holy Spirit.

OPTION 4: 1 Corinthians 6:13c-15a, 17-20
*This reading encourages us to remember that we were made for God, and it
is in God that we will flourish.*

Brothers and sisters:
The body is not for immorality, but for the Lord,
   and the Lord is for the body;
   God raised the Lord and will also raise us by his power.

Do you not know that your bodies are members of Christ?
Whoever is joined to the Lord becomes one spirit with him.
Avoid immorality.
Every other sin a person commits is outside the body,
   but the immoral person sins against his own body.
Do you not know that your body
   is a temple of the Holy Spirit within you,
   whom you have from God, and that you are not your own?
For you have been purchased at a price.
Therefore glorify God in your body.

OPTION 5: 1 Corinthians 12:31-13:8a

St. Paul's words encourage us to persevere in love. He assures readers that when love is patient, kind, and rejoices with the truth, it endures all things.

Brothers and sisters:
Strive eagerly for the greatest spiritual gifts.

But I shall show you a still more excellent way.

If I speak in human and angelic tongues
  but do not have love,
  I am a resounding gong or a clashing cymbal.
And if I have the gift of prophecy
  and comprehend all mysteries and all knowledge;
  if I have all faith so as to move mountains,
  but do not have love, I am nothing.
If I give away everything I own,
  and if I hand my body over so that I may boast
  but do not have love, I gain nothing.

Love is patient, love is kind.
It is not jealous, is not pompous,
  it is not inflated, it is not rude,
  it does not seek its own interests,
  it is not quick-tempered, it does not brood over injury, it does not rejoice
    over wrongdoing
  but rejoices with the truth.
It bears all things, believes all things,
  hopes all things, endures all things.
Love never fails.

OPTION 6: Ephesians 4:1-6

In this reading, St. Paul encourages us to live the best life that we can, to embrace our own journey, and to bear with one another through love.

Brothers and sisters:
I, a prisoner for the Lord,
  urge you to live in a manner worthy of the call you have received,
  with all humility and gentleness, with patience,
  bearing with one another through love,
  striving to preserve the unity of the Spirit
  through the bond of peace: one Body and one Spirit,
  as you were also called to the one hope of your call;
  one Lord, one faith, one baptism;
  one God and Father of all,
  who is over all and through all and in all.

*OPTION 7: Ephesians 5:2a, 21-33 (long form) OR Ephesians 5:2a, 25-32
(short form)
*Husbands are asked to lay down their entire lives for their wives, and wives
are encouraged to show love and respect for their husbands.*

Brothers and sisters:
Live in love, as Christ loved us
  and handed himself over for us.

Be subordinate to one another out of reverence for Christ.
Wives should be subordinate to their husbands as to the Lord.
For the husband is head of his wife
  just as Christ is head of the Church,
  he himself the savior of the body.
As the Church is subordinate to Christ,
  so wives should be subordinate to their husbands in everything.
Husbands, love your wives,
  even as Christ loved the Church
  and handed himself over for her to sanctify her,
  cleansing her by the bath of water with the word,
  that he might present to himself the Church in splendor,
  without spot or wrinkle or any such thing,

that she might be holy and without blemish.
So also husbands should love their wives as their own bodies.
He who loves his wife loves himself.
For no one hates his own flesh
 but rather nourishes and cherishes it,
 even as Christ does the Church,
 because we are members of his Body.

For this reason a man shall leave his father and his mother
 and be joined to his wife,
and the two shall become one flesh.

This is a great mystery,
 but I speak in reference to Christ and the Church.
In any case, each one of you should love his wife as himself,
 and the wife should respect her husband.

OR

Brothers and sisters:
Live in love, as Christ loved us
 and handed himself over for us.

Husbands, love your wives,
 even as Christ loved the Church
 and handed himself over for her to sanctify her,
 cleansing her by the bath of water with the word,
 that he might present to himself the Church in splendor,
 without spot or wrinkle or any such thing,
 that she might be holy and without blemish.
So also husbands should love their wives as their own bodies.
He who loves his wife loves himself.
For no one hates his own flesh
 but rather nourishes and cherishes it,

even as Christ does the Church,
because we are members of his Body.

For this reason a man shall leave his father and his mother
  and be joined to his wife,
and the two shall become one flesh.

This is a great mystery,
  but I speak in reference to Christ and the Church.

OPTION 8: Philippians 4:4-9
This is an invitation to rejoice, and encouragement to have no anxiety if
we put God at the center of our lives. He brings us joy when we focus on
whatever is true, honorable, just, pure, lovely, and gracious.

Brothers and sisters:
Rejoice in the Lord always.
I shall say it again: rejoice!
Your kindness should be known to all.
The Lord is near.
Have no anxiety at all, but in everything,
  by prayer and petition, with thanksgiving,
  make your requests known to God.
Then the peace of God that surpasses all understanding
  will guard your hearts and minds in Christ Jesus.

Finally, brothers and sisters,
  whatever is true, whatever is honorable,
  whatever is just, whatever is pure,
  whatever is lovely, whatever is gracious,
  if there is any excellence
  and if there is anything worthy of praise,
  think about these things.
Keep on doing what you have learned and received

and heard and seen in me.
Then the God of peace will be with you.

OPTION 9: Colossians 3:12-17
This reading celebrates a life of character and virtue. It talks about the greatest virtue of love and encourages us to invite Jesus to bring peace and love into our hearts.

Brothers and sisters:
Put on, as God's chosen ones, holy and beloved,
  heartfelt compassion, kindness, humility, gentleness, and patience,
  bearing with one another and forgiving one another,
  if one has a grievance against another;
  as the Lord has forgiven you, so must you also do.
And over all these put on love,
  that is, the bond of perfection.
And let the peace of Christ control your hearts,
  the peace into which you were also called in one Body.
And be thankful.
Let the word of Christ dwell in you richly,
  as in all wisdom you teach and admonish one another,
  singing psalms, hymns, and spiritual songs
  with gratitude in your hearts to God.
And whatever you do, in word or in deed,
  do everything in the name of the Lord Jesus,
  giving thanks to God the Father through him.

OPTION 10: Hebrews 13:1-4a, 5-6b
Marriage is something worth celebrating and holding in high esteem. Marriage is at its best when both husband and wife seek help in God.

Brothers and sisters:
Let mutual love continue.
Do not neglect hospitality,

for through it some have unknowingly entertained angels.
Be mindful of prisoners as if sharing their imprisonment,
and of the ill-treated as of yourselves,
for you also are in the body.
Let marriage be honored among all
and the marriage bed be kept undefiled.
Let your life be free from love of money
but be content with what you have,
for he has said, *I will never forsake you or abandon you.*
Thus we may say with confidence:

The Lord is my helper,
and I will not be afraid.

*OPTION 11: 1 Peter 3:1-9
This reading talks about how true beauty is not found on the outside, but
within. It encourages us to exercise compassion and to be a blessing for
one another through our conduct.

Beloved:
You wives should be subordinate to your husbands so that,
even if some disobey the word,
they may be won over without a word by their wives' conduct
when they observe your reverent and chaste behavior.
Your adornment should not be an external one:
braiding the hair, wearing gold jewelry, or dressing in fine clothes,
but rather the hidden character of the heart,
expressed in the imperishable beauty
of a gentle and calm disposition,
which is precious in the sight of God.
For this is also how the holy women who hoped in God
once used to adorn themselves
and were subordinate to their husbands;
thus Sarah obeyed Abraham, calling him "lord."

You are her children when you do what is good
  and fear no intimidation.

Likewise, you husbands should live with your wives in understanding,
  showing honor to the weaker female sex,
  since we are joint heirs of the gift of life,
  so that your prayers may not be hindered.

Finally, all of you, be of one mind, sympathetic,
  loving toward one another, compassionate, humble.
Do not return evil for evil, or insult for insult;
  but, on the contrary, a blessing, because to this you were called,
  that you might inherit a blessing.

OPTION 12: 1 John 3:18-24
Life is full of challenges, but God will always help when we follow his
commandment to love one another "in deed and truth."

Children, let us love not in word or speech
  but in deed and truth.

Now this is how we shall know that we belong to the truth
  and reassure our hearts before him
  in whatever our hearts condemn,
  for God is greater than our hearts and knows everything.
Beloved, if our hearts do not condemn us,
  we have confidence in God
  and receive from him whatever we ask,
  because we keep his commandments and do what pleases him.
And his commandment is this:
  we should believe in the name of his Son, Jesus Christ,
  and love one another just as he commanded us.
Those who keep his commandments remain in him, and he in them,

and the way we know that he remains in us
is from the Spirit that he gave us.

OPTION 13: 1 John 4:7-12
This passage encourages us to love one another because God loved us. We receive this gift of love from God and participate in it by loving others.

Beloved, let us love one another,
  because love is of God;
  everyone who loves is begotten by God and knows God.
Whoever is without love does not know God, for God is love.
In this way the love of God was revealed to us:
  God sent his only-begotten Son into the world
  so that we might have life through him.
In this is love:
  not that we have loved God, but that he loved us
  and sent his Son as expiation for our sins.
Beloved, if God so loved us,
  we also must love one another.
No one has ever seen God.
Yet, if we love one another, God remains in us,
  and his love is brought to perfection in us.

OPTION 14: Revelation 19:1,5-9a
This reading is from the last book of the Bible. It captures John's vision of the wedding feast of the Lamb, of Jesus at the end of time. It is a beautiful way to see how marriage ultimately points us to heaven.

I, John, heard what sounded like the loud voice
  of a great multitude in heaven, saying:

  "Alleluia!
  Salvation, glory, and might belong to our God."

A voice coming from the throne said:

"Praise our God, all you his servants,
and you who revere him, small and great."

Then I heard something like the sound of a great multitude
or the sound of rushing water or mighty peals of thunder,
as they said:
"Alleluia!
The Lord has established his reign,
our God, the almighty.
Let us rejoice and be glad
and give him glory.
For the wedding day of the Lamb has come,
his bride has made herself ready.
She was allowed to wear
a bright, clean linen garment."
(The linen represents the righteous deeds of the holy ones.)

Then the angel said to me,
"Write this:
Blessed are those who have been called
to the wedding feast of the Lamb."

ALLELUIA VERSE

The Alleluia Verse, or Gospel Acclamation, is said or sung by the priest, deacon, or cantor. It prepares us to receive the Word of God in the Gospel.

OPTION 1: 1 John 4:7b
Everyone who loves is begotten of God and knows God.

OPTION 2: 1 John 4:8b and 11
God is love;
Let us love one another, as God has loved us.

OPTION 3: 1 John 4:12
If we love one another,
God remains in us
and his love is brought to perfection in us.

OPTION 4: 1 John 4:16
Whoever remains in love,
remains in God and God in him.

OPTION 5: Psalm 134:3
May the LORD bless you from Zion,
he who made both heaven and earth.

GOSPEL

The Gospel reading is a story of Jesus' life and ministry from one of the four Gospels: Matthew, Mark, Luke, or John. It is read by the priest or deacon.

OPTION 1: Matthew 5:1-12a
This passage captures Jesus' Sermon on the Mount. He gives a beautiful and powerful vision of a life well lived in the famous Beatitudes.

When Jesus saw the crowds, he went up the mountain,
   and after he had sat down, his disciples came to him.
He began to teach them, saying:

"Blessed are the poor in spirit,
  for theirs is the Kingdom of heaven.
Blessed are they who mourn,
  for they will be comforted.
Blessed are the meek,
  for they will inherit the land.
Blessed are they who hunger and thirst for righteousness,
  for they will be satisfied.
Blessed are the merciful,
  for they will be shown mercy.
Blessed are the clean of heart,
  for they will see God.
Blessed are the peacemakers,
  for they will be called children of God.
Blessed are they who are persecuted for the sake of righteousness,
  for theirs is the Kingdom of heaven.
Blessed are you when they insult you and persecute you
  and utter every kind of evil against you falsely because of me.
Rejoice and be glad,
  for your reward will be great in heaven."

OPTION 2: Matthew 5:13-16
Jesus tells his disciples they can have an incredible impact on the world and the people around them if they boldly live out their faith.

Jesus said to his disciples:
"You are the salt of the earth.
 But if salt loses its taste, with what can it be seasoned?
 It is no longer good for anything
  but to be thrown out and trampled underfoot.
 You are the light of the world.
 A city set on a mountain cannot be hidden.
 Nor do they light a lamp and then put it under a bushel basket;

it is set on a lamp stand,
    here it gives light to all in the house.
Just so, your light must shine before others,
    that they may see your good deeds
    and glorify your heavenly Father."

OPTION 3: Matthew 7:21, 24-29 (long form) OR Matthew 7:21, 24-25 (short form)
Jesus tells the parable of a man who built his house on rock and a man who built his house on sand. A marriage that puts God at the center is a marriage built on rock.

Jesus said to his disciples:
"Not everyone who says to me, 'Lord, Lord,'
    will enter the Kingdom of heaven,
    but only the one who does the will of my Father in heaven.

"Everyone who listens to these words of mine and acts on them
    will be like a wise man who built his house on rock.
The rain fell, the floods came,
    and the winds blew and buffeted the house.
But it did not collapse; it had been set solidly on rock.
And everyone who listens to these words of mine
    but does not act on them
    will be like a fool who built his house on sand.
The rain fell, the floods came,
    and the winds blew and buffeted the house.
And it collapsed and was completely ruined."

When Jesus finished these words,
    the crowds were astonished at his teaching,
    for he taught them as one having authority,
    and not as their scribes.

OR

Jesus said to his disciples:
"Not everyone who says to me, 'Lord, Lord,'
    will enter the Kingdom of heaven,
    but only the one who does the will of my Father in heaven.

"Everyone who listens to these words of mine and acts on them
    will be like a wise man who built his house on rock.
The rain fell, the floods came,
    and the winds blew and buffeted the house.
But it did not collapse;
    it had been set solidly on rock."

*OPTION 4: Matthew 19:3-6
Marriage is forever. In this reading, Jesus is questioned about divorce, and he responds saying, "what God has joined together, man must not separate."

Some Pharisees approached Jesus, and tested him, saying,
    "Is it lawful for a man to divorce his wife for any cause whatever?"
He said in reply, "Have you not read that from the beginning
    the Creator made them male and female and said,
    *For this reason a man shall leave his father and mother
    and be joined to his wife, and the two shall become one flesh?*
So they are no longer two, but one flesh.
Therefore, what God has joined together, man must not separate."

OPTION 5: Matthew 22:35-40
Love is a beautiful thing. And it is our calling. When someone asks Jesus what the greatest commandment is, he replies that the greatest commandment is to love God with all your heart, soul, and mind, and the second is to love your neighbor as yourself.

One of the Pharisees, a scholar of the law, tested Jesus by asking,
"Teacher, which commandment in the law is the greatest?"
He said to him,
"You shall love the Lord, your God,
with all your heart,
with all your soul,
and with all your mind.
This is the greatest and the first commandment.
The second is like it:
You shall love your neighbor as yourself.
The whole law and the prophets depend on these two commandments."

*OPTION 6: Mark 10:6-9
Jesus celebrates the beauty of the union between man and woman in marriage,
and stresses that what God has joined together no one must separate.

Jesus said:
"From the beginning of creation,
God made them male and female.
For this reason a man shall leave his father and mother
and be joined to his wife,
and the two shall become one flesh.
So they are no longer two but one flesh.
Therefore what God has joined together,
no human being must separate."

*OPTION 7: John 2:1-11
Jesus performs his first miracle at a wedding. His act of turning water into
wine symbolizes how God gives in abundance to those who have faith and
believe in his goodness.

There was a wedding in Cana in Galilee,
and the mother of Jesus was there.
Jesus and his disciples were also invited to the wedding.

When the wine ran short,
the mother of Jesus said to him,
"They have no wine."
And Jesus said to her,
"Woman, how does your concern affect me?
My hour has not yet come." His mother said to the servers,
"Do whatever he tells you."
Now there were six stone water jars there for Jewish ceremonial washings,
each holding twenty to thirty gallons.
Jesus told them,
"Fill the jars with water."
So they filled them to the brim.
Then he told them,
"Draw some out now and take it to the headwaiter."
So they took it.
And when the headwaiter tasted the water that had become wine,
without knowing where it came from
(although the servants who had drawn the water knew),
the headwaiter called the bridegroom and said to him,
"Everyone serves good wine first,
and then when people have drunk freely, an inferior one;
but you have kept the good wine until now."
Jesus did this as the beginning of his signs in Cana in Galilee
and so revealed his glory,
and his disciples began to believe in him.

OPTION 8: John 15:9-12
As he prepares to leave his disciples and ascend into Heaven, Jesus tells them that the path to complete joy is to love one another as he has loved them. He encourages them (and us) to remain in his love.

Jesus said to his disciples:
"As the Father loves me, so I also love you.
Remain in my love.

If you keep my commandments, you will remain in my love,
    just as I have kept my Father's commandments
    and remain in his love.
"I have told you this so that my joy might be in you
    and your joy might be complete.
This is my commandment: love one another as I love you."

OPTION 9: John 15:12-16

There is no greater love than laying down your life for a friend. Christ laid down his life for us, demonstrating the love of God. Husbands and wives are called to love as Christ loved us by sacrificing for one another and by living selflessly.

Jesus said to his disciples:
"This is my commandment: love one another as I love you.
No one has greater love than this,
    to lay down one's life for one's friends.
You are my friends if you do what I command you.
I no longer call you slaves,
    because a slave does not know what his master is doing.
I have called you friends,
    because I have told you everything I have heard from my Father.
It was not you who chose me, but I who chose you
    and appointed you to go and bear fruit that will remain,
    so that whatever you ask the Father in my name he may give you."

OPTION 10: John 17:20-26 (long form) OR John 17:20-23 (short form)

Jesus desires that we will know the love of God the Father and that we will be with him in Heaven. Through your love for one another, you and your spouse will strive to bring each other closer to God and closer to Heaven.

Jesus raised his eyes to heaven and said:
"I pray not only for my disciples,
    but also for those who will believe in me through their word,

so that they may all be one,
as you, Father, are in me and I in you,
that they also may be in us,
that the world may believe that you sent me.
And I have given them the glory you gave me,
so that they may be one, as we are one,
I in them and you in me,
that they may be brought to perfection as one,
that the world may know that you sent me,
and that you loved them even as you loved me.
Father, they are your gift to me.
I wish that where I am they also may be with me,
that they may see my glory that you gave me,
because you loved me before the foundation of the world.
Righteous Father, the world also does not know you,
but I know you, and they know that you sent me.
I made known to them your name and I will make it known,
that the love with which you loved me
may be in them and I in them."

OR

Jesus raised his eyes to heaven and said:
"I pray not only for my disciples,
but also for those who will believe in me through their word,
so that they may all be one,
as you, Father, are in me and I in you,
that they also may be in us,
that the world may believe that you sent me.
And I have given them the glory you gave me,
so that they may be one, as we are one,
I in them and you in me,
that they may be brought to perfection as one,
that the world may know that you sent me,
and that you loved them even as you loved me."

Appendix

FREQUENTLY ASKED QUESTIONS ABOUT CATHOLIC WEDDINGS

Why get married in a Catholic church?

In a time when it seems that everyone around you may be busy planning a wedding on the beach, in a barn, or in some other setting, you may be asking yourself, "Why do we have to get married in a Catholic church?"

Even though you are celebrating your wedding in the presence of your friends and family, the ceremony is more than a social event. Marriage was created by God to be sacred. Marriage belongs to him.

As such, the Church requires Catholics to celebrate their wedding in a Catholic church with a priest and two witnesses. Because marriage is a covenant made before God and the Church, we make this commitment in a church.

If you or your fiancé is not Catholic, it may be possible to celebrate your wedding in a non-Catholic church or in a different location. However, you will need to receive special diocesan permission to do so. And it will be important to work with your local parish to ensure that the requirements for the Catholic person are fulfilled.

What does it mean to say that marriage is a sacrament?

Jesus gave us the sacraments as outward ways to pour grace into our lives. When you partake in a sacrament, it is more than just a ceremony – you actually receive grace and blessing from God. Marriage between two baptized persons is a sacrament because the man and the woman enter a covenant with one another and with God. Their exchanging of vows makes the marriage a sacrament.

Can we be validly married in the Catholic Church if one of us is baptized non-Catholic?

Yes. A valid Catholic marriage is one in which the spouses are free to marry, freely exchange their consent in the presence of two witnesses and an authorized Church minister, and commit to a lifelong marriage that is faithful and open to children. A Catholic and non-Catholic Christian can be validly married in the Church with permission from the local bishop. Your priest or deacon can help you through the process of acquiring permission. And the Church offers a ceremony, or Rite of Marriage, that can be adapted to recognize your situation.

Can we be validly married in the Catholic Church if one of us is not baptized?

Yes. The Church offers a ceremony, or Rite of Marriage, for you. You will still have prayers, readings, the exchange of vows, and a blessing. While not sacramental, the marriage between a Catholic and a non-baptized individual is still valid in the eyes of the Church with permission from the local bishop. Your priest or deacon can help you through the process of acquiring permission.

What happens during the ceremony if only one of us is Catholic?

The Church recommends using the Rite of Celebrating Marriage Without Mass if you both are baptized but only one of you is Catholic.

With approval from your bishop, the Rite of Marriage Within Mass may be celebrated – however, the non-Catholic spouse would not be able to receive Holy Communion. Therefore, the Rite of Celebrating Marriage Without Mass may be more appropriate and inclusive, especially if a large number of your guests are also not Catholic.

If one spouse is not baptized, the Rite of Celebrating Marriage Between a Catholic and a Catechumen or non-Christian is used.

Your priest or deacon can provide guidance as you decide which rite to use.

Who can receive Holy Communion at the wedding?

Receiving Communion at a wedding is a beautiful moment.

Communion means "in union with." When you receive Communion, you are proclaiming your union with the beliefs of the Catholic Church, including the belief that the bread and wine become the Body and Blood of Jesus. This is a marvelous sign of unity.

The Church desires to ensure that all who receive the Eucharist, which serves as a sign and source of unity, are truly in union with the teaching. Regrettably, divisions still exist among Christian groups. For example, many Christians do not share our understanding that the Eucharist is the presence of Christ himself. Because of these divisions, inter-communion is not permitted.

For this reason, when one of the partners is not Catholic, it may be preferable to use the rites that do not include the Mass. This decision may help avoid misunderstanding.

How will our non-Catholic guests know what is going on during the ceremony?

In order to help your guests follow along, you may want to print and distribute programs that explain the different parts of the ceremony. This will be especially helpful if you are having a full Mass. Ask your parish if they have an existing template to guide you in creating a program.

Who do we involve in the ceremony?

If you plan on having a full Mass (see page 1), you will need a priest to officiate and lead the liturgy. If you would like to include more than one priest, you may invite additional priests to celebrate the Mass alongside the main priest. It is common etiquette to gain pastoral approval from the parish priest if you would like to have more than one priest. If your wedding ceremony will not include Mass (see page 31), you can ask a deacon to officiate.

The Church requires two witnesses to be present during the ceremony. The best man and maid/matron of honor normally serve as your primary two witnesses.

You may also invite friends and family to be a part of the ceremony in other ways. This is a wonderful way to include them in your special day. Your priest can provide guidance in determining how best to incorporate your guests.

Normally, you will want to have the following roles at your wedding ceremony:

FOR A CEREMONY WITH MASS:

Priest
Ushers
Eucharistic ministers
Readers
Cantors
Altar servers
Gift bearers

FOR A CEREMONY WITHOUT MASS:

Priest or deacon
Ushers
Readers

Do the people in our wedding have to be Catholic?

The Church asks that only baptized Catholics serve as altar servers and Eucharistic ministers. Altar servers and Eucharistic ministers perform sacred duties and have special training provided by the Church.

If you are using the Rite of Celebrating Marriage Within Mass (see page 1), the individuals proclaiming the readings should be Catholic. If you are using the other two rites, your readers do not need to be Catholic.

No matter which rite you use, the members of the wedding party do not need to be Catholic.

How do we choose which music to include during the ceremony?

The music selections available will largely depend on the parish and the Music Director's preferences. Many parishes will already have lists of wedding music, which will greatly aid you in making your choices. Keep in mind the goals and dreams you have for your marriage when selecting the music, and bring the same intentionally here as you did for the readings and prayers. Since the ceremony is essentially one long prayer, the music should also be prayerful and sacred in nature. There is a wide variety of beautiful hymns that speak of the love God has for you and the love you share with your spouse. Be sure to schedule a meeting with the Music Director to receive help in determining the best songs to use.

Depending on the parish and which form of the Rite of Marriage you use, you may need to select music for the following:

- Prelude music (your church may have standard songs they use for this)
- Seating of grandmothers and mothers
- Processional (wedding party, priest/deacon, altar servers, etc.)

- Bridal entrance
- General Mass settings (Gloria; Holy, Holy; Lamb of God)
- Offertory (when gifts of bread and wine are presented)
- Communion hymn
- Marian dedication (optional, see below)
- Recessional

Can we include readings from sources other than the Bible?

God speaks to us through the Scriptures. That is why The Order of Celebrating Matrimony calls for the use of Scripture readings. For weddings, the Church provides a number of options from Scripture that speak about the sacramental nature of marriage and covenant love. Those options have been provided earlier in this booklet so that you can choose the readings for your ceremony.

You may choose to utilize non-biblical texts that are meaningful to you and your fiancé outside the ceremony itself. For example, you may print them in your program or incorporate these in the wedding reception.

Can we write our own vows?

The Church has crafted the vows in the Rite of Marriage with intentionality. These vows reflect the promises and duties of husband and wife. While vows are personal expressions of your love for one another, they are shared publicly in a formal ceremony and cannot be uniquely written by the couple. To be married, a bride and groom each promise to:

- take one another as their lawfully wedded spouse
- be faithful to one another in good times and in bad (for better or for worse and for richer or for poorer)
- be faithful to one another in sickness and in health
- love, honor, and cherish one another all the days of their lives

The vows provided by the Church include all of these promises.

If you would like to share personal stories about your relationship and your dreams for your marriage, you may want to do so during the reception.

What is the Universal Prayer? How do we write our own intercessions?

The Universal Prayer, also called the Prayer of the Faithful, is a beautiful opportunity to pray for others. You and your spouse are able to work with your priest or deacon to write intercessions that are important to you.

Your priest or deacon will likely also be able to provide pre-written intercessions for you to use if you prefer.

What other traditions can we incorporate in the ceremony?

There are several ethnic and cultural traditions that may or may not be included in *The Order of Celebrating Matrimony*. Your priest or deacon will be able to provide guidance regarding any additional rituals you would like to include in your ceremony.

Marian Dedication
Many couples ask for Mary's help and guidance in their marriage. As Jesus' mother, Mary guides us to Jesus in a very unique and beautiful way.

A Marian dedication typically consists of presenting a bouquet of flowers at the foot of a statue of Mary before the final blessing. You may take a brief moment to silently pray a Hail Mary or another short prayer together. A Marian hymn such as "Ave Maria" is usually played or sung at this time.

Can we light a *unity candle during the ceremony?*

Generally, parishes prohibit lighting a unity candle because it is not included in *The Order of Celebrating Matrimony*. Candles are meant to signify the light of Christ, whereas a unity candle typically signifies two becoming one. This message is already conveyed through the exchange of vows. Therefore, the union it symbolizes will still be very present in your ceremony. If you would like to incorporate a unity candle in your wedding, you may want to have one during the reception.

HELPFUL WISDOM FOR YOUR MARRIAGE

The following featured articles are from *The 21 Undeniable Secrets of Marriage* by Dr. Allen Hunt. To request a FREE copy, go to DynamicCatholic.com/21Secrets.

The Secret of Bedrock

For a marriage to work, it is important to share everything, including the deepest values in your heart.

The secret of bedrock may perhaps be the greatest gift I can give you.

Plenty of research shows that this secret will be the strongest predictor of the success of your marriage. Priests and pastors will recommend that any relationship start with it. Without the secret of bedrock, your foundation will be unsteady. It may last, but it will always have wobbles in the structure that will prevent your marriage from standing strong and steady, as you deeply yearn for it to do.

What is the secret of bedrock? Prayer. Prayer that leads to a spiritual life together as a couple. A spiritual life together that will give you the same values and convictions in your heart so that the two of you are driving your relationship in the same direction at the same time in all settings. A deep melding will bind you together as a couple, and that bond will sustain you in ways you can never anticipate at the beginning. Your shared spiritual life will serve as mortar between the bricks of your home, pulling all the various parts together and holding them together as a unified whole.

When your child does not come home one night as expected and you aren't sure how to react, the secret of bedrock will see you through. When you are unable to have children on your own, the secret of bedrock will steady your love for one another and guide you. When your husband gets laid off from his job, or is diagnosed with cancer, the secret of bedrock will be your friend. Most of all, when you face major decisions as a couple, the secret of bedrock will remind you both of what you really value and what ultimately matters, because you believe the same things. You hold the same things dear.

Virtually every study ever done has shown that couples who share the same faith, and practice that faith together, have the lowest rates of divorce. That does not mean that all other marriages will fail, only that they are less likely to stand the test of time and trial. In America, it is increasingly challenging to find a mate who shares your faith and practices it in the same you do. We have grown increasingly secular and hostile toward religion. We've also grown so multicultural that many people are unwilling to set down deep roots in any one faith and set of beliefs. Instead, they lead their lives as a sampler of many cultures, never sinking deeply into any set of commitments or values.

A University of Texas at San Antonio study found that couples who shared their faith and worshipped together regularly not only reported a higher level of marital satisfaction but also raised that satisfaction level even further when they were active together in other ways at their church. Most of all, when the couples shared prayer and devotional practices at home, their marital satisfaction level ranked the highest of any participants in the study of 1,387 couples.

Add to that a University of Virginia study that found that merely attending worship together as a couple reduces the divorce rate by about 35 percent. Stronger still, a Georgia Family Council survey showed that of couples who prayed together, only 7 percent had seriously ever considered divorce, compared to 65 percent of those who never prayed together. You get the point.

In an era when the length of celebrity marriages is measured in hours and days and the divorce rate is usually quoted as about 50 percent, one thing is clear: Marriage is hard. And when you do not have the same core beliefs, and you do not see your life and the world in the same way, marriage is even harder. In fact, it's almost impossible.

Our own research at the Dynamic Catholic Institute found that when both spouses actively practice their Catholic faith together, the divorce rate is less than 11 percent. In other words, your marriage is almost guaranteed to thrive when you go to Mass, give generously, serve compassionately, and pray together.

When you do those things regularly rather than sporadically, you drop your likelihood of disaster from 50 percent to 11 percent. That's a nearly 80 percent shrinkage in the divorce rate—just from actively practicing your faith together. Shared faith plus shared convictions equals strong marriage. Pretty good results, huh?

For a marriage to work, it is important to share everything, including the deepest values in your heart. Your relationship with God lies at the center of who you are and shapes all you do. When you and your spouse do not share that, you are trying to sing a duet from two different song sheets.

The book of Tobit does not get much airtime in Mass during the year, but in it, you will find a beautiful jewel to remind you of the secret of bedrock. When Tobiah learns that God has chosen Sarah to be his wife, he immediately falls in love with her, without ever having seen her in person. He places his faith in God above all else. His relationship and marriage are placed in the hands of God.

Sarah has been betrothed before. In fact, she's been there six times before! And each time, her husband-to-be was slain by a demon on the wedding night. Six times in a row. Not good.

Nevertheless, in spite of this track record, Tobiah trusts in God and His plan. He marries Sarah despite the dangers he's been warned of by every other observer. When the newlyweds face the fear of their wedding night and the proximity of demons, danger, and death, they immediately turn first to the Lord. They get on their knees and pray together.

Tobiah rose from bed and said to his wife, "My sister, come, let us pray and beg our Lord to grant us mercy and protection."

She got up, and they started to pray and beg that they might be protected. He began with these words:

> "Blessed are you, O God of our ancestors;
> blessed be your name forever and ever!
> Let the heavens and all your creation bless you forever.
> You made Adam, and you made his wife Eve
> to be his helper and support;
> and from these two the human race has come.
> You said, 'It is not good for the man to be alone;
> let us make him a helper like himself.'
> Now, not with lust,
> but with fidelity I take this kinswoman as my wife.
> Send down your mercy on me and on her,
> and grant that we may grow old together.
> Bless us with children."
> They said together, "Amen, amen!"
> Then they went to bed for the night.

(TOBIT 8:4–9)

Their relationship is rooted in faith. God lies at the bedrock of the marriage. Tobiah tests his motives for marriage before God: May this relationship be built on faith and fidelity rather than on lust and immaturity. Their marriage not only survives the wedding night, but this beautiful prayer becomes a template for all marriages to follow. Faith and fidelity create marriages built to last.

When you have children, the challenges become even more pronounced. Schedules get tighter, money gets scarcer, kids get older and begin making their own decisions, and the list goes on. The secret of bedrock becomes even more important for your marriage and family. First, you have less attention to pay to one another as a couple. Sharing the same view of God and life will equip you for this season of marriage when you have less time for each other. Second, you will now have little souls who are counting on you to prepare them for life. Only you can grow them into the people God wants and designed them to be. The secret of bedrock will help you build faith into your home life and into your children's souls.

You may choose to build a tradition with your children during Advent to get ready for Christmas. Traditions create meaning and consistency in your family. Long after your children are grown, they will still remember—and often ask to do—the traditions, whether they are lighting an Advent wreath in your home together or serving at the homeless shelter as a family each Thanksgiving.

You could decide to devote a week's vacation each year to serving on a mission team through your parish. You might build a habit of daily prayer and Bible or devotional reading into your home so that your children learn sound spiritual habits. The secret of bedrock can also be expressed like these words from Saint Paul in Colossians 3: "Whatever you do, do it all in the name of the Lord Jesus."

When you build these spiritual habits into your marriage, family, and life, you will create a home that can stand in even the strongest storm. In a way you will become like a man named Tho Bien, who immigrated to America from Vietnam. He married a woman from Germany, and they moved into the California hills and began to build their dream home.

Tho Bien did all the work himself. He poured the foundation. He did the framing. He put the roof in place. He laid the plumbing lines and put in the electrical wiring. Tho Bien did it all. For two years, he labored, buying only the best materials for his work. He wanted his home to be excellent. And he put stucco on the outside to make it fireproof.

When the wildfires came to their area, Tho Bien was ready. Everyone else evacuated their homes. He sent his wife and daughter away, but he stayed with the house he had built. Most of the time, he sat on the roof, pouring water on it to keep it damp and cool. Tho Bien had invested so much of himself in that house that he could not bear to abandon it.

Today, if you go to that area, you will find a hillside ravaged and charred. You will find no trees. Only a few chimneys and toilet bowls remain near the top of the hill. You will also find Tho Bien and his family still living in the dream house he built by hand with only the finest materials. In a way, Tho Bien is like the man Jesus described who built his house upon the rock rather than on the sand. When the storms came, his house stood tall and strong.

When you establish your marriage on the shared values of your faith, and then regularly practice that faith together, you will be stormproofing your life and family. That doesn't mean you will not face challenges; it merely means you will have the strength and depth of resources to weather them.

God is not some vague, distant force to people who pray regularly, but rather a personal friend and adviser. These people are trying to listen to the voice of God in their lives. They know that doing God's will is the only path that leads to lasting happiness in this changing world (and in the world beyond). What is important to recognize is that dynamic Catholics have a time to pray, a place to pray, and a structure to their prayer.

The most straightforward way to do this springs forth from our Dynamic Catholic Prayer Process. When you as a couple develop a prayer habit—it may be as simple as five to ten minutes per day—your marriage will thrive in a way you could never have anticipated. New strengths will emerge, and God will begin to open vistas on your future and your family. Again, the point is to make a simple habit—five to ten minutes a day. An occasional, sporadic prayer here and there ("Oh, Lord, help me find a parking space," or "Oh, Lord, help us get home in this storm") is not a bad thing. But a regular prayer habit is something altogether different. You're pouring the foundation for your life together.

Daily prayer is your relationship with God. Without it, there really is no relationship. With no communication, it is difficult to have any relationship, especially a divine one. And when you pray together as a couple, you are inviting God's grace into your life, and His spirit to grow you both forward. Remember, you are helping each other get to heaven.

Here are the basics of the Prayer Process that our team at Dynamic Catholic uses and suggests:

1. GRATITUDE

Begin by thanking God in a personal dialogue for whatever you are most grateful for today.

2. AWARENESS

Revisit the times in the past twenty-four hours when you were and were not the-best-version-of-yourself. Talk to God about these situations and ask him to give you the gift of greater awareness when similar situations arise in the future.

3. SIGNIFICANT MOMENTS

Identify something that you experienced today and explore what God might be trying to say to you through that event.

4. PEACE

Ask God to forgive you for any wrong you have committed (against yourself, another person, or Him) and to fill you with a deep and abiding peace.

5. FREEDOM

Talk to God about how He is inviting you to change your life so that you can experience the freedom that comes from knowing that who you are, where you are, and what you are doing makes sense. Is He inviting you to rethink the way you do things? Is God asking you to let go of something or someone? Is He asking you to hold on to something or someone?

6. PRAY FOR OTHERS

Pray for those you feel called to pray for today, and those who have asked you to pray for them recently. Take a moment and pray for these people by name, asking God to bless and guide them.

FINISH BY PRAYING THE OUR FATHER.

Slowly build this simple little habit into your daily life as a couple, and open yourself to a wellspring of God's presence. Then watch as that presence guides you through the roller coaster of experiences that every marriage brings. Best of all, watch that wellspring of your prayer life bear fruit in the lives of your family and children. You will build your house upon the rock.

That is the secret of bedrock.

The Secret of Priorities

Every marriage will face a turning point.

Life is about priorities. Love is about priorities. And a marriage thrives when it embraces the secret of priorities.

Show me your calendar or phone and I'll show you your priorities. When you make time for something, it becomes your priority. Where you invest your time is where you are investing yourself. Show me your bank statement and I'll show you your priorities. When you spend money or give money, your heart becomes attached and that project or item becomes a priority. After all, Jesus said, "Where your treasure is, your heart will follow." (Matthew 6:21) Your heart follows your money.

When I was sixteen, I desperately pined for a car. I asked my dad if I could have a car. He said, "Sure, son, just as soon as you figure out how to pay for it." So I went to work. I decided not to play baseball in high school so I could work to afford a car. Purchasing that car became my priority. I organized my life around it. Finally, after lots of hard work, I had saved enough to buy myself a very used Volkswagen Rabbit. It was a bit rusty, but it ran. It leaked, so I had rainwater in my back floorboard whenever the storms came. Girls certainly were impressed by that unintentional foot-washing device. But it was my car. I owned it. I had purchased it with my own money. I bought the gas and paid for the upkeep.

After buying that car in high school, I spent most Saturdays washing that jalopy. I became expert at painstakingly creating the greatest luster and shine on the old green Rabbit. I spent still more time applying Armor All to the tires and to the interior of the car so they sparkled. That car became my priority. In order to say yes to that car, I said no to baseball, I said no to trips to the beach with friends, I said no to anything that would consume money or time that I needed for my car. The car was my priority. That's where my time and my money went.

When your priorities change, your life changes in the same direction.

I was enamored of that car for several years, until my interest cooled a bit. I found other things that were more interesting to me, like girls. They also required money and time. My priorities changed. And how I used my time and my money changed.

Eventually, I moved on to another car, and then another. I barely remember that first car now. It was my priority for a while, but things changed. Life moved on. I developed new priorities—because after all, it was only a car, right?

You get the point. If getting a new job is your priority, you will spend time getting the education and experience you need, and networking to make the contacts necessary to acquire that new job. That's your priority.

If recreation is your priority, you will allocate free time in your schedule for that extra round of golf or to spend time at the lake. You will adjust your budget to trim other costs so that more money is available for your recreational pleasure.

When your priorities change, your life changes in the same direction. When your relationship and marriage are your priority, then you will adjust your time and your money to reflect that. Some couples start off with the priority like I had with my first car. They spend all their time together, and they spend most of their money together. But eventually the interest cools. He may find himself investing more time in golf and his poker buddies. She may have outlets with her friends at work or in the neighborhood. Slowly, the couple begins merely to coexist. A slight distance sets in. That distance grows slowly but surely each year, sometimes peacefully, sometimes not so much, for the rest of the relationship.

However, you and I believe that God has created marriage for most of us as the primary way by which we will be transformed into the-best-version-of-ourselves—our holiest, most saintly selves. And we believe that God's love is made known to us in powerful ways in our marriage when we allow it to happen. If you believe these things are true, your marriage will be your priority for the rest of your days. Should your priorities change, expect real shifts to occur in your marriage. That is the secret of priorities.

One word the Church uses to capture the secret of priorities is covenant. God initiates a covenant. God's covenant revolves around His steadfast and exclusive love for His people. God is faithful and His covenant is unbreakable. It is a commitment, and it is God's priority. We base marriage on that example.

God's covenant begins in the Old Testament with His relationship with His chosen people of Israel. He initiates that covenant with Abraham and then with Moses. "I will be your God, and you will be my people." (Exodus 19:5ff)

Israel strays from God and disobeys Him time and time again. Nevertheless, God still remains faithful to His promises. He continues to call His people back to Himself. His covenant is unbreakable, and God will be faithful.

Jeremiah captures God's never-failing love and persistence when he writes what God told him: "'This is the covenant I will make with the house of Israel after that time,' declares the Lord. 'I will put my law in their minds and write it on their hearts. I will be their God and they will be my people . . . I will forgive their wickedness and remember their sins no more.'" (Jeremiah 31:33–34)

This is a God for whom the covenant is a priority. He does not waver. He continues to pursue and to love.

Finally, God extends that covenant to the entire world in Jesus. His love and faithfulness are no longer focused only on Israel. As Jesus eats with His disciples for the last time in the upper room, He shares, "This cup is the new covenant in my blood, which is poured out for you." (Luke 22:20)

When God describes a covenant, He is not thinking about a simple contract or an agreement to hang out together as long as both He and we enjoy it. God's covenant involves unwavering love expressed in the sacrifice of His own Son, who is willing to die in order to bring us home. That covenant includes regular nourishment in the Eucharist and regular communication in prayer. Now that covenant is a priority.

Similarly, the Church teaches that marriage is a covenant. A covenant is unbreakable. And covenants take priority. That is one of the reasons why couples who live together before they marry are far more likely not to marry at all, and if they do, they are more likely to divorce than couples who do not live together. The "test drive" argument does not work because living together lacks the very heart of a covenant marriage. You do not stumble or ease into a marriage. Rather, you make a deep commitment. Priority.

Marriage may be the last modern institution based on covenant, and even that appears to be an endangered species in our culture now. We humans like convenience and disposability far more than we do covenants and unbreakable promises that are reliably and honorably kept. But deep down, you and I know what is good for us. Actually, we know what is best for us. We are at our best when we are faithful rather than reckless. We become more holy when we keep our promises rather than break them. We are most proud when we persist rather than quit. And we are most joyful when we are fully loving and being loved rather than always looking for the next good thing, which usually turns out to be as unsatisfying as the last thing or relationship we tried.

God's idea of a covenant is an unbreakable, everlasting commitment, a non-negotiable promise. That concept came to my mind several years ago when I walked into a funeral home to visit one of my friends whose grandmother had died. As I entered the parlor, I saw the grandmother's body lying in the casket. Next to the casket sat her husband, my friend's grandfather, in his wheelchair. He had lifted her arm from the casket in order to hold her hand as he greeted the handful of visitors stopping by to offer him comfort. From his wheelchair, he gently caressed her hand and mentioned to each visitor that he and she had been just a few days shy of their sixtieth anniversary when she died. Years ago, he had made a nonnegotiable promise. For better, for worse, until death do us part. Covenant.

That is what God has in mind because it leads us to be our best selves. The marriage covenant does not shackle us. Just the opposite—it frees us to realize our full potential. The covenant unleashes a new dimension of love.

In that way, perception determines behavior. When you perceive marriage as a covenant created by God, unbreakable and everlasting, that perception changes your behavior. Your marital covenant takes priority. You invest yourself and your resources in this special promise. And that new behavior creates destiny. You will discover new portions of yourself and your own capacity to grow and love because you have committed yourself to this divinely ordained covenant. You will move toward the-best-version-of-yourself through this covenant as you and your spouse help each other get to heaven. Perception determines behavior. Behavior then determines destiny.

Focusing on what God has in mind pays far more dividends in life than focusing merely on what I might want at any given moment. After all, at one moment when I was younger, I let my heart get attached to an old, rusty car. That is why the Church teaches that marriage is a covenant.

Covenants take priority. Priorities require time, they require effort, and they usually require money. Best of all, marriages are worth every bit of it.

That is the secret of priorities.

Covenants take priority.

The following featured articles by Matthew Kelly are drawn from the Everyday Life section of DynamicCatholic.com. Everyday Life provides hundreds of articles on topics including relationships, health and wellbeing, work and career, marriage and sexuality, and money matters. These articles are designed to help you become the–best-version-of-yourself. To learn more, visit DynamicCatholic.com.

———————————

3 Reasons Why God Wants You to Have a Great Sex Life

The culture around us seems to be either obsessed with sex or fearful of it. But in spite of prevalent unhealthy views about sex, the truth is that God designed sex to not just be good, but great! Here are three reasons He wants you to have a fantastic sex life:

1. **GOD MADE YOU FOR INTIMACY.**

   The intimacy you enjoy with your spouse is a taste of the union you are meant to have with God.

   Human beings were created male and female, with bodies designed to fit together. Sex is the closest we can get to another person body and soul. Because of its power to bond us together and to bring forth new life, God intended sex for marriage. In a committed, exclusive relationship, a man and a woman can grow in unity with one another over their years together. Sexual intimacy is a big part of that. The intimacy you enjoy with your spouse is a taste of the union you are meant to have with God.

2. GOD WANTS YOU TO BE HEALTHY.

God's dream for each of us includes being as healthy as we can be. Sex can help! Studies show that human touch is crucial to our well-being—in fact, an infant cannot survive without touch and as we grow older, we still need it. The health benefits of sex go well beyond touch, however. Sex improves our health in similar ways that exercise does—by boosting the immune system, lowering blood pressure, and improving heart health. Studies have linked sex to better sleep, lower stress levels, and even pain relief. Some researchers believe it can also reduce the risk of prostate cancer and help bladder control in women. Sex improves mood and enhances well-being, providing emotional and psychological benefits. What's not to like about all that?

3. GOD WANTS YOU TO BE HAPPY.

There are other ways God could have arranged for us to propagate our species, of course, but he made it so that humans had to unite sexually to create new life. There's probably no better evidence to show the gift God meant sex to be than how pleasurable it is. And pleasure makes us happy. It's not simply that our bodies experience sexual activity as pleasurable, but all that happens before, during, and after sex that contributes to that pleasure—the physical affection and emotional intimacy, the release of endorphins, and the experience of loving and being loved.

Sex isn't something we should ever hide from God—instead it is part of his plan to help us be the best-version-of-ourselves in our marriages. God wants you to have a healthy, vibrant sex life. Don't be afraid to strive for it!

The Best Marriage Advice Ever

Richard Paul Evans seemed to have it all—five beautiful kids, a gorgeous home in Utah, and a successful career as a New York Times bestselling author. But he wasn't happy. His marriage was in terrible shape and his struggles with his wife, Keri, had only grown more difficult through the years. It got to the point where Richard looked forward to being away from home on book tours.

One night, after a long-distance fight on the phone that ended with Keri hanging up in mid-shout, Richard found himself in the shower of his hotel room yelling at God and crying out for help. Why had he married someone so different from him? Why couldn't she change? And then, in his despair, a profound realization came to him that ended up changing everything: He couldn't change his wife, he could only change himself.

If you want a better marriage, change yourself first.

It's true, isn't it? No matter how much you nag, cajole, plead, or pray for your spouse to change, the only person you really have the ability to change is you. Becoming the best-version-of-yourself will help you love your spouse and yourself in a new better way. As hard as change can be, there are plenty of resources to help you start. Perfectly Yourself is a favorite of mine.

Richard asked God to help him figure out how he could change. He was inspired to start focusing more attention on his wife and her needs, rather than on himself. So he went home and began to ask her every morning how he could make her day better. He kept doing it, day after day, week after week, and before long the walls between them began tumbling down, and their relationship became warmer, more intimate, and much more harmonious.

In his hotel room far away from home that night, and in the days and months after, Richard discovered what may just be the best marriage advice ever: If you want a better marriage, change yourself first.

If you take your focus off what your spouse needs to change and commit to changing yourself first, your marriage will be enriched in ways that may surprise you.

When you get serious about personal change, your marriage will change, too. Because as you begin to live more authentically, with greater humility, commitment and love, it has a powerful effect on all those around you, especially your spouse and those closest to you.

So how do you begin?

First, ask God for inspiration, guidance, and help. Then start with one concrete thing. Maybe, like Richard, you will decide to focus on your spouse each day, like doing something helpful, or saying three kind things. Or maybe you need to commit to something you know your spouse deeply wants you to do but you've been dragging your feet. Whatever it is, if you take your focus off what your spouse needs to change and commit to changing yourself first, your marriage will be enriched in ways that may surprise you.

If you take your focus off what your spouse needs to change and commit to changing yourself first, your marriage will be enriched in ways that may surprise you.

ADDITIONAL RESOURCES

Marriage is a lifelong journey – and yours is just beginning!

As you challenge and encourage each other to become the-best-version-of-yourselves, Dynamic Catholic wants to be a resource for you. Get the full Dynamic Catholic marriage experience to help you build a great marriage.

DynamicCatholic.com/BetterTogetherProgram

Invite God to guide you through the process.

SELECTION FORM:

RITE 1: THE ORDER OF CELEBRATING MATRIMONY WITHIN MASS

*Add your selections for the prayers and readings to this form and give to your priest or deacon. To fill out an electronic version and have it emailed to your priest or deacon, visit **DynamicCatholic.com/CeremonyForm***

BRIDE

Name (First and Last) _____

Email Address _____

Phone Number _____

GROOM

Name (First and Last) _____

Email Address _____

Phone Number _____

Name of Celebrating Priest or Deacon _____

Name(s) of Concelebrant(s) (if applicable) _____

Parish Name _____

Date and Time of Rehearsal _____

Date and Time of Celebration _____

Altar Servers (circle one): **We will provide   Parish will provide**

Number of Ushers/Greeters _____

Number of Bridesmaids and Groomsmen (combined) _____

Ring Bearers (circle one):   **Yes   No**

How many? _____

Flowergirls (circle one):   **Yes   No**

How many? _____

Musicians: ☐ **We will provide**   ☐ **Parish will provide**
                        ☐ **Combination of personal and parish musicians**

Has the Parish Music Director been contacted?

                        ☐ **Yes**   ☐ **No**

___

THE INTRODUCTORY RITE

ENTRANCE PROCESSION

☐ **Both bride and groom accompanied by parents, preceded by wedding party and presiding clergy**

☐ **Both bride and groom accompanied by parents, preceded by wedding party**

☐ **Bride accompanied by parents, preceded by wedding party**

☐ **Bride accompanied by father, preceded by wedding party**

☐ **Other:** _____ _____

Please circle your selection

COLLECT see pages 3–5

1   2   3   4   5   6

THE LITURGY OF THE WORD

FIRST READING see pages 6–7

1   2   3   4   5   6   7   8   9

Read by: _____

RESPONSORIAL PSALM see pages 7-8

1   2   3   4   5   6   7

Led by: _____

Read or sung? (circle one)   Read   Sung

SECOND READING see pages 8-9

1   2   3   4   5   6   7   8   9   10   11   12   13   14

Read by: _____

ALLELUIA VERSE see page 10

1   2   3   4   5

Led by: _____

Read or sung? (circle one)   Read   Sung

GOSPEL see pages 10-11

1   2   3   4   5   6   7   8   9   10

THE CELEBRATION OF MATRIMONY

CONSENT see pages 13-15

1   2   3   4

RECEPTION OF CONSENT see page 16

1   2

BLESSING AND GIVING OF THE RINGS see pages 16-17

1   2   3

BLESSING AND GIVING OF THE *ARRAS* see page 17

☐ Yes   ☐ No

THE LITURGY OF THE EUCHARIST

PRAYER OVER THE GIFTS see pages 18-19

1   2   3

Gifts brought forward by: _____

PREFACE see pages 19-21

1   2   3

BLESSING AND PLACING OF THE *LAZO* OR VEIL see page 21

                    ☐ **Yes**   ☐ **No**

NUPTIAL BLESSING see pages 21-27

Part I: 1   2   3   4
Part II: 1   2   3

note: If Option 2 is selected for the Collect, Option 1 of Part II of the Nuptial Blessing may not be used

PRAYER AFTER COMMUNION see pages 27-28

1   2   3

Who in the wedding party will be receiving Communion?

_____

_____

_____

THE CONCLUSION OF THE CELEBRATION

FINAL BLESSING see pages 28-30

1   2   3

Additional Notes:

Additional Notes:

SELECTION FORM:

RITE 2: THE ORDER OF CELEBRATING MATRIMONY WITHOUT MASS

*Add your selections for the prayers and readings to this form and give to your priest or deacon. To fill out an electronic version and have it emailed to your priest or deacon, visit **DynamicCatholic.com/CeremonyForm***

BRIDE

Name (First and Last) _____

Email Address _____

Phone Number _____

GROOM

Name (First and Last) _____

Email Address _____

Phone Number _____

Name of Celebrating Priest or Deacon _____

Name(s) of Concelebrant(s) (if applicable) _____

Parish Name _____

Date and Time of Rehearsal _____

Date and Time of Celebration _____

Number of Ushers/Greeters _____

Number of Bridesmaids and Groomsmen (combined) _____

Ring Bearers (circle one):   Yes   No

How many? _____

Flowergirls (circle one):   Yes   No

How many? _____

Musicians: ☐ We will provide   ☐ Parish will provide

☐ Combination of personal and parish musicians

Has the Parish Music Director been contacted?

☐ Yes   ☐ No

THE INTRODUCTORY RITE

ENTRANCE PROCESSION

☐ Both bride and groom accompanied by parents, preceded by wedding party and presiding clergy

☐ Both bride and groom accompanied by parents, preceded by wedding party

☐ Bride accompanied by parents, preceded by wedding party

☐ Bride accompanied by father, preceded by wedding party

☐ Other: _____

Please circle your selection

COLLECT see pages 33-35

1   2   3   4   5   6

THE LITURGY OF THE WORD

FIRST READING see pages 36-37

1   2   3   4   5   6   7   8   9

Read by: _____

RESPONSORIAL PSALM see pages 37-38

1   2   3   4   5   6   7

Led by: _____

Read or sung? (circle one)   Read   Sung

SECOND READING see pages 38-39

1   2   3   4   5   6   7   8   9   10   11   12   13   14

Read by: _____

ALLELUIA VERSE see page 40

1   2   3   4   5

Led by: _____

Read or sung? (circle one)   Read   Sung

GOSPEL see pages 40-41

1   2   3   4   5   6   7   8   9   10

THE CELEBRATION OF MATRIMONY

CONSENT see pages 43-45

1   2   3   4

RECEPTION OF CONSENT see page 46

1   2

BLESSING AND GIVING OF THE RINGS see pages 46-47

1   2   3

BLESSING AND GIVING OF THE *ARRAS* see page 47

☐ Yes   ☐ No

BLESSING AND PLACING OF THE *LAZO* OR VEIL see page 48

☐ **Yes**   ☐ **No**

NUPTIAL BLESSING see pages 48-53

Part I: 1   2   3   4

Part II: 1   2   3

note: If Option 2 is selected for the Collect, Option 1 of Part II of the Nuptial Blessing
may not be used

COMMUNION **(Optional)**

☐ **Yes**   ☐ **No**

Who in the wedding party will be receiving Communion?

_____

_____

_____

THE CONCLUSION OF THE CELEBRATION

FINAL BLESSING see pages 54-56

1   2   3

Additional Notes:

Additional Notes:

SELECTION FORM:

RITE 3: THE ORDER OF CELEBRATING MATRIMONY BETWEEN A CATHOLIC AND A CATECHUMEN OR NON-CHRISTIAN

*Add your selections for the prayers and readings to this form and give to your priest or deacon. To fill out an electronic version and have it emailed to your priest or deacon, visit **DynamicCatholic.com/CeremonyForm***

BRIDE

Name (First and Last) _____

Email Address _____

Phone Number _____

GROOM

Name (First and Last) _____

Email Address _____

Phone Number _____

Name of Celebrating Priest or Deacon _____

Name(s) of Concelebrant(s) (if applicable) _____

Parish Name _____

Date and Time of Rehearsal _____

Date and Time of Celebration _____

Number of Ushers/Greeters _____

Number of Bridesmaids and Groomsmen (combined) _____

Ring Bearers (circle one):   Yes   No

How many? _____

Flowergirls (circle one):   Yes   No

How many? _____

Musicians: ☐ We will provide   ☐ Parish will provide
                  ☐ Combination of personal and parish musicians

Has the Parish Music Director been contacted?
           ☐ Yes   ☐ No

THE INTRODUCTORY RITE

ENTRANCE PROCESSION

☐ Both bride and groom accompanied by parents, preceded by wedding party and presiding clergy

☐ Both bride and groom accompanied by parents, preceded by wedding party

☐ Bride accompanied by parents, preceded by wedding party

☐ Bride accompanied by father, preceded by wedding party

☐ Other: _____

Please circle your selection

THE LITURGY OF THE WORD

FIRST READING see pages 59-60

1   2   3   4   5   6   7   8   9

Read by: _____

RESPONSORIAL PSALM see page 61

1   2   3   4   5   6   7

Led by: _____

Read or sung? (circle one)   Read   Sung

SECOND READING see pages 61-63

1   2   3   4   5   6   7   8   9   10   11   12   13   14

Read by: _____

GOSPEL see pages 63-64

1   2   3   4   5   6   7   8   9   10

THE CELEBRATION OF MATRIMONY

CONSENT see pages 66-68

1   2   3   4

RECEPTION OF CONSENT see page 69

1   2

BLESSING AND GIVING OF THE RINGS see pages 69-70

1   2   3

BLESSING AND GIVING OF THE *ARRAS* see page 70

☐ Yes   ☐ No

BLESSING AND PLACING OF THE *LAZO* OR VEIL see page 71

☐ Yes   ☐ No

Additional Notes: